Ballads of the Great West

With line drawings by
GLEN ROUNDS

Ballads
of the
Great West

Edited with commentary by

Austin & Alta Fife

173646

AMERICAN WEST PUBLISHING COMPANY

PALO ALTO / CALIFORNIA

Contents

Ballads
of the
Great West

Edited with commentary by

Austin & Alta Fife

173646

AMERICAN WEST PUBLISHING COMPANY

PALO ALTO / CALIFORNIA

Library of Congress Card Number 70-119002
ISBN 0-910118-17-5

For
STEPHEN FIFE LANGDON
to blaze his trail west

Contents

PART II

The Cowboy and
Other Western Types   69

PART III

Dramatic Situations and Events   127

PART IV

Code of the Cowboy 177

Preface

O UR INTEREST in folk and primitive poetry of the American
West stems from a broad and sustained interest in all
of the folk expressions of Anglo-American pioneers on the
frontier: tales and anecdotes of pioneer experience; sayings,
proverbial expressions, jingles, and rhymes transformed and
transplanted to the West by its European intruders; arts, crafts,
and the folk technology used to establish, sustain, and enrich
life in a vast and lonely environment; beliefs, superstitions,
rites, practices, and other aspects of personal or social life which
gave cohesiveness to an otherwise chaotic society; and especially
the ballads, songs, and other verse which westerners transplanted
and reshaped to the needs of the unique experience and new
modes of being, imposed upon them by a unique environment.

As for the West's folk and primitive verse, it is both difficult
and meaningless to separate it from the ballads and songs, many
of which have enjoyed a dual life as songs that have floated in
oral tradition and also as verse published in newspapers, farm
and cattlemen's journals, and other popular or esoteric imprints.
Inversely, many of the poems, though originally conceived as
verse and published in sundry popular vehicles, have been taken
over by singers of and for the folk and, wedded thus to tradi-
tional or newly created melodies, have become an integral part
of the popular musical repertoire of the American West. There
are also cases where the original author established the meter of
his poem to make it singable to a favorite traditional tune.

The body of verse from which this selection was extracted
is vast, and the sources extremely varied. Several hundred poems
have been examined, and from one to a score of variants of each.

This raises at once the question of criteria followed in the selection or rejection of items. While we are quite ready to admit that the editors' subjective judgment played a primary role, we have tried to keep certain qualities in mind. Has the poem floated in oral tradition or appeared widely in popular imprints? Does it depict everyday human values, the clichés of a culture, the attitudes and viewpoints of the "folk"? Do form and style conform to traditional popular standards? Do the mythic views of the folk culture supplant therein the individualized concepts of a single human being? Can unsophisticated readers perceive and react to its central meanings without help from college hill? Can a particular poem be read and its content be fully perceived without knowledge of its author's biography and other works? If a "yes" answer applied to all or most of the questions above, then we felt the poem worthy of presentation as a specimen of folk or primitive verse.

Authorship has not been used as a criterion for selection: in most cases texts of the poems selected came into our possession before the authors were identified, since popular vehicles of transmission for this kind of literature seldom affix the name of an author. Nevertheless, having once made our selections, we have tried to determine authorship and give credit wherever possible. We apologize to authors whom we have failed to credit for want of corroborating evidence.

And who are these authors? Unsophisticated, anonymous participants in the western experience? Often. Westerners with a "mite of learnin'" — even a college degree — a love of the West and a talent for myth perception and myth making? Frequently. Finished, non-western or western poets inspired by the drama, pathos, heroism, and humor of the Westward Movement? Occasionally, but only when their intense individuality gave way to identification with the mass of humanity on the western frontier.

Establishing the best text for each poem has been difficult, especially with the most "folksy" of these poems, as these have undergone multiple changes in the processes of popular transmission, and each may possess several to a score of widely differing texts. In all cases, however, we have used integral texts and have allowed ourselves editorial license just sufficient to give the poem its full meaning. Even defective punctuation and spelling have been preserved except where they seemed to vitiate the meaning of the poem or to make reading unnecessarily difficult.

Full bibliographical data on our sources is given with each poem. Texts encountered in inaccessible or esoteric places have been assembled in the bound volumes of the Fife American Collection (FAC) or the Fife Mormon Collection (FMC), comprising:

FAC or FMC I: items collected directly from oral sources.

FAC or FMC II: items collected from manuscript sources.

FAC or FMC III: items collected from esoteric printed sources.

Gordon: two volumes extracted from the Robert W. Gordon Collection at the Library of Congress.

Gordon-Oregon: one volume extracted from the Robert W. Gordon Collection at the University of Oregon.

Hendren: seven volumes from the manuscript collection of Stella M. Hendren of Kooskia, Idaho.

JL: three volumes extracted from the manuscript collection of John A. Lomax in the archives of the Texas Historical Society, Austin.

PC-F: one volume from the collection of Edwin Ford Piper at the State University of Iowa.

PNFQ: three volumes from the manuscript collection of the Pacific Northwest Farm Quad, Spokane, Washington.

We wish to express our gratitude to informants, friends, and professional colleagues who have given assistance and support in the preparation of this work. Especially we thank D. Wynne Thorne, vice president for research; Allen W. Stokes, ornithologist; and Arthur H. Holmgren, botanist, all of Utah State University.

It has been challenging and exciting to collect and collate these lyrical expressions of the moods and experiences of Anglo-Americans in the West. If even a small portion of that exciting adventure can be transmitted to the readers, then our purpose will have been achieved.

AUSTIN AND ALTA FIFE

Introduction

Cowboy "Lingo"
and the Western Setting

T HE NEW ENVIRONMENT and life-styles in the American West were more than the frontiersmen's inherited English language could cope with. Terrain and climate, new biological forms, North American Indians and Hispanic-Americans of the Southwest, and especially new modes of being imposed upon Anglo-Americans by the new environment, made demands upon the language beyond its Old World images. It is precisely among these new phenomena that there emerge the stereotypes, characteristic images, mythical prototypes, and situations which came to be felt as "western."

First, there was the physical environment itself, with its vast prairies, its arid expanses swept by dust storms and cyclones, its ruddy *mesas* and deep *arroyos*, its moody rivers — now dry and now surging torrents — its expanses of alkali pocked with mirages for the disheartened wanderer, its prairie fires.

Then there were the animals of the West which loomed as a

15

threat to man's dominion—bison, elk, moose, grizzly bear, wild mustangs, antelope, mountain sheep, wolves, rattlesnakes, and the clever coyote—desert and mountain denizens to be destroyed and replaced by domestic strains familiar and subservient to our European forebears long before there was an America or a "West." Sharing the same environment was a host of botanical forms as strange and foreboding as the terrain and the animals: sagebrush, cacti, mesquite, soaproot, joint grass, and tumbleweeds.

This exotic domain was inhabited by human "varmints" as rough, as awesome, as undisciplined, as varied in their origins, aspect, and mores as were the setting, the animals, and the plants. Each has been stereotyped in the poetry with his costume, his manner, and his social role as sharply drawn as for puppets at the *Grand Guignol.* The Indian is drawn as fierce, bloodthirsty, crafty, untrustworthy, mean, stupid; or else noble, majestic, and heroic when confronted with the white man's aggression and intransigeance (stereotypes rarely conform either to reason or to facts). The Hispanic-American male, or "greaser," is viewed as a pitiful, mean, and lazy creature, almost subhuman. Indian and Mexican women are pretty, provocative, and enamoured of the Anglo-American cowboys: "Lasca" throwing her body over her cowboy lover to shield him from the hooves of stampeding cattle, or a bewitching Mexican beauty betraying father and faith to accompany Bill Roy to Cheyenne. Strangely enough, there is no stereotype for the American Negro; he is not often encountered, but when he is it is in roles that are honorable if humble, and occasionally even heroic.

Several stereotypes of Anglo-American westerners emerge. They behave in simple and predictable ways, though not so simply that classification merely as "good guys" and "bad guys" is adequate. The prospector is a loner, a simple dreamer. He appears in town from time to time with mule and pack, only to vanish among the thorns and sage when he has renewed his store of grub; or he empties his pouches of gold on the bar, buys drinks for the house, scatters his precious ore in the saloon girls' laps, and then goes back to the wilderness. A stranger to the immediate community is portrayed as the tenderfoot, to be humiliated, tested, or hazed before acceptance by the new group; or as an evil seducer who gets what the local boys were after and then vamooses unpunished. Also to be included here is the genuine westerner's conception of the Hollywood or dude-ranch hands, who "set" a guitar better than they do a horse, and haze women better than they do cattle.

Texas Rangers, Mounties, and soldiers who staffed the frontier outposts are cast typically in a heroic mold, as are their civilian guides: Carson, Cody, Bridger, and others. (You may believe that Mexican border ballads draw a different picture!)

Underdogs are omnipresent in this literature: the youth whose witchy stepmother has driven him west; the remorseful young man fleeing a crime of passion; the frail gunman who sets a bully back on his heels.

The outlaw sometimes appears as a Robin Hood who defies the law and its restriction on human freedoms, stealing from the rich and giving to the poor, astutely evading and bedeviling the lawman, his dash, swagger, and ingenuity atoning for moral or ethical lapses. Less often he appears simply as an unredeemed criminal. Frequently dramatic confrontations develop in which the outlaw Robin Hood and the unredeemed variety are pitted against each other, in which case the outcome is seldom in doubt. Frontier justices of the peace have also evolved as stereotypes: ignorant Sancho Panza–like characters, clever, venal, but redeemed by showmanship.

As a mythic type, the cowboy, of course, enjoys ascendancy over all the others. He is known over the earth wherever western movies, phonograph records, American radio and television shows, rodeos and wild West shows, dime novels, funnies, pulp magazines, or farm, horse, or cattlemen's journals have circulated. The type is not an easy one to characterize because it has several faces, the "cowboy" being, in effect, a synthesis of the "western American" generally. His costume and working gear are unique and provocative. He is a man of quick decision, action, dash, daring, and toughness; a man who prefers to live freely and dangerously rather than to chafe under the constraints of social institutions. He can, notwithstanding, give way to reverie, thoughtful silence, and transcendental speculation. He has learned to live with loneliness, and the simple conviviality of a few "pards" has more value than carousal in a trail's end saloon, though he can become rowdy and gregarious, a natural-born prankster. When he hits a trail-end town, he wrangles cards, alcohol, and women in the same rough-shod but honest way he punches cattle, though sometimes there are prickings of conscience, and typically the girls and cardsharks fleece him. Like the plague he scorns elegance — in dress, talk, and manner — and cultivates the rough qualities of the out-of-doors. In moments of over-stimulation (alcoholic, that is) he boasts like a man treed by malign nature or human cussedness. There may be several women in his life, but seldom more than three who count for aught but evil: his sweetheart, his sister, and his mother. All human contacts and all values are dwarfed by allegiance to these women whose role in his life is not unlike that of the Virgin Mary (or Lady Gwendolyn) in the lives of the knights of thirteenth-century Europe. Sweethearts often prove false, yet his allegiance does not waver.

There are other female images which loom in the poetry of cowboys and the West: the loyal and rugged frontiersman's wife; the girl male-impersonator whose disguise is revealed ultimately when she shoots down the dastard who killed her lover; the agile Pony Express rider whose feminine gender is disclosed only when an Indian arrow is extracted from her bosom. Nor should we forget the Indian maidens or *señoritas* from south of the border whose devotion to an Anglo-American lover leads them to elope, abandoning the wealth and name of their Latin grandee sires; or the bewitching Latin beauty who entices and rebuffs. Grass in the other pasture . . .

There are also the female outlaws, the dance-hall belles, and occasional female images conceived to provoke laughter by their nonconformity to the cowboy fixation that women are *per se* beautiful and good. Any cowboy would risk death or self-abasement to shield the honor of a woman, even though honor she had not.

In moments when the cowboy is not submerged in a life of action, we see him as nostalgic: nostalgic for the home and family he has left behind; nostalgic especially for the good old frontier of his youth, which he now sees being transformed by sodbusters, railroads, fences, automobiles and highways, telegraph and telephone, into a world whose softness and order he does not relish. The West itself looms in the cowboy's heart as an eerie thing, a land of the magical, the ideal, the attained and lost, the to-be-sought-but-not-found over-the-horizon of the past or of the future. And the cowboy, despite his obvious deviations, maintains a basic respect for religion and, though seldom seen in church, is rarely an infidel.

The dependence of the cowboy on his mount is basic to the western image. The winning of the West looms as the last great achievement made by men on horseback. The metallic logic of steam and combustion are shortly to displace the sinews, the biological warmth of horses. When his cavvy is threatened with death in the flames of a prairie fire, the *Wrangler Kid* risks his own life to save it. A cowboy's brashest boast is to ride and break an unridden outlaw horse, and no moments are so intense in his life as are those spent on the back of a bucking bronco.

He is not always a winner: like *Roland* of the era of epic poetry, he is also magnificent (or merely human) in his defeats. Outlaw horses throw him fifty ways from Sunday; a puncher on a new-fangled contrivance (bicycle) beats him to a fare-thee-well.

Cowboy nicknames are themselves often manifestations of the new culture. Saddle bum that he is, he is often known merely by the state whence he came ("Tex," "Utah") or by the state plus an epithet ("Nevada Red," "Montana Kid"). He may be called by a physical or moral trait which he has, or by its opposite ("Slim," "Tiny," "Parson"). Or his "moniker" may include the brand of the ranch for which he works ("V-Bar Bill," "Circle S John"). Strong loyalties are notable between punchers of the same outfit, and equally excessive hatreds for outsiders.

The image of the camp cook, on trail or roundup, appears from time to time. He is typically a seasoned but "stove-up" cowboy whose ill-mended injuries or other infirmities make riding and punching impossible. There is often a healthy rivalry between him and the punchers, and he may use his control of the food to lord it over them. Meanwhile the trail boss, touted in the western movies, is rarely encountered.

Stereotyped Cowboy and
Western Situations and Images

CERTAIN EXPERIENCES, episodes, events, and circumstances are treated recurrently in this literature, and in a stereotyped and magnificent manner as in legend or myth. Let us identify some of the most characteristic ones since, taken together, they provide the subject matter for a large part of the folk and primitive poetry of the West. One cluster of images surrounds the circumstances and modes of travel to and in the West: the river boats; migration around the Horn or through Panama; the Pony Express; freighting by ox team, mules, or horses; stagecoaches; covered wagons; and the ultimate arrival of railroads.

Many of the cowboy's chores with respect to the management of cattle appear as dramatic illuminations, too, often with symbolic overtones: the herds themselves; the bedground, night herding, and cow camps; the cattle drives with treacherous river-crossings and mad stampedes; rounding-up, roping, and branding; range wars; prairie fires; storms; floods; buffalo hunting. Gun-play is typical in street or saloon, in rocky *arroyo*, or on the trail, and is often accompanied by bragging, bullying, threats, or other dramatic confrontations. Death and burial on the prairie or in the sundry "Boot Hills" of frontier towns was, quite naturally, as frequent and as dramatically compulsive as was gun-play.

Code of the Cowboy

IN DISCUSSING SONGS, ballads, poetry, tales, proverbs, and other verbal expressions of the folk, critics have frequently spoken of the "code" of the people who share this oral or popular literature. Hence there has been talk about the "code of the cowboy," though we are not aware that anyone has ever tried, systematically, to define it. The task is not an easy one, but we shall attempt a few generalizations, aware that the folk and popular poetry of the West is only one of several media which give pertinent insights, and also that the cowboy cult is but one of several streams through which the westerner's code is projected. Our statement will comprise his notions about God and the natural order, the social order, and the nature of individuality. One should not, of course, expect the cowboy code to comprise a full explanation of the nature of man and the cosmos or a system void of contradictions. Folk expressions do not offer answers for all philosophical questions, but only for those which confront man in a compelling and self-evident way. Nor does their "code" necessarily form a coherent system, not logic but analogy being man's particular genius.

Frontiersmen inherited from Judeo-Christian tradition the belief in a Supreme Being who behaves more or less like an idealized human. He reigns over the worldly order of life, but more particularly over life in the hereafter. Apart from his vague role as creator and master of existence, his intercession in the affairs of men is exceptional rather than routine: miracles are possible but rare. By and large, man must carve out his own destiny. The devil appears, though infrequently and most typically in a ludicrous role; he is a kind of anticreator, ready and eager to detect the flaw by which a soul may be induced into his kingdom in the afterlife. Christianity is taken for granted; religion is respected though active participation in its rituals or other institutionalized manifestations is not universal nor indispensable. Preachers are generally respected, and blasphemy rigorously punished.

Good and evil, right and wrong, are clear-cut issues and self-evident. There are few gray areas where the choices a man has to make are difficult, and the real issue is having the will power to make the right decisions, evil so often having a cussed kind of lure about it. To get into God's kingdom in the afterlife, happily, all your choices don't have to be right; but the crucial ones do, especially those made when the ride over the "Last Divide" is imminent. In any case, "salvation" is not viewed as an immediate goal but rather as a natural end product of the good life.

If God is generally good, benevolent, and merciful, nature is not. Climate, storm, drought, flood, pestilence, and terrain; "varmints" and subhuman humans — all conspire to bedevil and challenge man. Malign nature is an obstacle against which the fiber of personal worth is tested, and ultimately the frontier — jousting arena for this encounter — is beloved not for bounty given gratuitously but for a pittance surrendered to the toil, sacrifice, and perseverance of man. By her feminine qualities — coyness, the art of provocation, vacillation between surrender and flight, sometimes harsh cruelty — nature in the West has exercised a magical compulsion over men, sufficient to give thousands of grim communities such a halo as to make each one (for its own) the "best damn town on earth."

In the code of the cowboy the stability and cohesiveness of society depend upon steadfastness in one's duty and honor between men, not upon civic or religious institutions toward which this literature frequently expresses either indifference or hostility. It follows, hence, that the cowboy is against lawmen — sheriff, judge, railroad "bull" — and is often sympathetic toward antisocial types such as bums, jailbirds, outlaws, saddle bums, and roustabouts, who defy, if not the law, at least its enforcement

22

officers. The Texas Rangers and Canadian Mounties are notable exceptions, though at times even they come in for a sound drubbing. Victims of legal, social, or economic institutions are objects of sympathy and often play heroic roles.

The cowboy code holds in disfavor "greasers" (a name used to identify Mexican males), most Indians, "Chinamen," the dude or tenderfoot, bullies, unredeemed badmen, and the perpetrators of blasphemy. Meanwhile Mexican and Indian women, some Indian warriors, and an occasional Negro cowboy are loved, admired, and respected.

Of all the phenomena of life, womanhood is the most worthy of love, respect, fear, and even worship. It is sacred in nearly all of its manifestations: mother, sweetheart or wife, sister or daughter, even the prostitute—in that relative order of intrinsic worth. All women are beautiful, and merely to evoke the image of an ugly woman is a cause for laughter or vengeance.

Discounting mother and sisters, a cowboy only loves once, but with a love that is overpowering, everlasting, and violent. The object of one's love obliterates all other female images. Though the western lover may once have dallied with other women (with prostitutes, mostly, since the respect due other women did not admit intimacies), once smitten by true love he becomes monogamous—oblivious, almost, to the existence of other women. Marriage, of course, is the inevitable goal and the sooner the better, once the shafts of love have hit their mark. Crimes of passion are pardonable. For women, true love is so all-embracing that they will deny blood or creed to follow the beloved male, even though he be a scoundrel.

In the choice of a wife, a member of one's own community and station is far safer than dazzling beauties from the city, or the provocative maidens in whose veins flow blood of exotic races. But admonitions to avoid their likes are all in vain, since love, especially in these circumstances, strikes like a plague: there is no preventive and no cure. In cases of seduction the male is *de facto* responsible, and vengeance by husband, brother, or father is mandatory.

In the lore of cowboys and other westerners, man is dual: body and soul. The latter transcends death and in its postmortal state lives on, enjoying many of the pleasures and none of the tribulations which we must bear on earth. There are vague allusions to damnation and hell, but rarely do men live a life so as to be eternally damned. Still, death is a tragedy, especially for the young — a kind of sub-rosa admission that mortality, even under adverse conditions, is better than whatever comes thereafter.

The social roles of men and women are sharply drawn. Man is tough of mind and muscle. His first duty is to his job. He has a kind of inner burning for adventure which drives him west despite the protests of ladies left behind. Or it may be that a crime, a youthful indiscretion, or the lure of gold has forced him to seek freedom, anonymity, or affluence in the West. He gives way to moving comradeships and to violent hatreds for other men, and sufficiently provoked, he is hasty to take the law into his own hands. By precept and by conscience he has learned that cards, whiskey, and harlots are evil; still he indulges these vices whenever duty or chance push him from the ranges and into the saloons of a frontier city, the size of his bankroll frequently determining the intensity and duration of his spree.

Prosody, Style, and Form

T HE POETRY OF THIS ANTHOLOGY comes from men of diverse talents, often through popular channels of transmission, and thus with inevitable alterations wrought by either subconscious or willful acts of those involved in the transmission process. So, it becomes difficult to make sweeping generalizations about prosody and style without providing for exceptions and particular deviations from the typical. In some cases our texts are fresh from the pens of sophisticated authors; in others, and perhaps most typically, they come from copies, or copies of copies, printed in sundry popular literature, written in notebooks, or handed down through oral transmission.

Although these poems are presented under the rubric of "folk" or "primitive," we note notwithstanding at least three different kinds of poems having some common stylistic features and some that are peculiar to each. These are bona fide folk and popular poems written by unpretentious and typically unknown poets who have something to say and who say it in the most direct and natural way they can. The story counts for everything, and spontaneously, perhaps even unconsciously, traditional poetic forms have been used as a vehicle for the all-important content. Second, there are poems by articulate and sophisticated poets who achieve a folk or primitive effect by sheer artistry. They have been moved by the "westernism" in the air about them, sensed its metaphoric and mythic potential, and verbalized these sensations as an artist might have painted them. Finally, there are poems with a burlesque flavor which capture and portray "westernism" by willful exaggeration of unpolished or uneven quality, but still provocative and titillating, like a Rabelaisian anecdote or a *fabliau*.

grass-roots primitive or folk

>For Belle was a beautiful tough one
>>And she led all her gang to the grave
>But while they were up and kickin'
>>Each one of them was her slave.

artistically primitive

>Go gather a load of the white, white salt
>>(Two cowboys all alone)
>For the salt lies wide and the salt lies free
>On the dry earth-bed of an ancient sea
>>There by the Cimarron.

burlesqued primitive

>To this ornery guy with the shifty eye
>>She uttered her favorite line,
>"You low down slicker, your breath smells of likker,
>>And your lips shall NOT touch mine!"

We have already said that content dominates form. This content is typically narrative or sentimental. Even in play-party or square dance calls there is a tendency to tell a story, or at least to relate a simple anecdote, or to describe a mood in terse, orderly, and natural language. In conformity to the above, a poem begins characteristically in simple direct narrative. Occasionally a single line or two is sacrificed to place the action in a geographic environment, in the personal context of the speaker's own life, or in the life of the protagonist. Sometimes there is a minstrel-like invitation to the listeners to give attention to the narrator's story. Or, the beginning lines may forewarn the listeners concerning the inevitable results of certain kinds of behavior, promising a narrative to clinch the point. Occasionally the opening lines announce or anticipate the culmination of the narrative, or imply a moral to become explicit in the subsequent narrative.

The poems end most typically with action or sentiment which is a natural conclusion, the inevitable climax, to the narrative. Typical endings consist of the death of the protagonist, burial by interested survivors, and sometimes the visit of the beloved to the burial site. Several of the poems end in an exhortation to the listener to take cognizance of the moral or other implications of the story, or in a resolve by the narrator to mend his ways. Often the poem ends with a nostalgic resolve to return to mother, sweetheart, and erstwhile home, or with the discovery on the corpse of a memento of home and loved ones. Frequently these poems end in a conventional formula or termination consisting of a kind of summation or terse restatement of theme, or pertinent moral precept. Occasionally the conclusion consists of an assertion concerning the truthfulness of the story, or a prayer of gratitude for some miraculous deliverance. In several of the poems, especially those of the "artistically primitive" variety, we note endings where the central theme is magnified into mythical proportions, a halo of the frontier era is cast upon the present, or, in less sophisticated pieces, lines in which the cowboy and the punching of cattle become symbols of God and of his dealings with men.

In the poems examined, a basic rhythmic group consisting of four metric feet seems to be by all odds the most frequent. These appear rhymed in various ways or as octasyllabic couplets with a caesura after the fourth foot and rhymed *a a, b b*.

26

"In for- | mer times," | said Bill, | "a man
Jest had | to be | more sub- | tile than
The sis- | sified | and sick- | ly jays
Of these | plumb tame, | downtrod- | den days.

Beside | that tent | and un- | der guard ||
    in ma- | jesty|alone | he stands
As some | chained ea- | gle, bro- | ken-winged, ||
    with eyes | that gleam | like smoul- | dering brands

The longer narrative poems generally use the eight-foot lines, no doubt because the burden of rhyme-making is reduced by one half. "Feminine" rhymes (i.e., of words stressed on the penultimate syllable) are relatively uncommon; but when they do appear, and especially when alternated neatly with masculine rhymes, the hand of an "educated feller" is apparent.

    The dying mule, the dried- | up spring,
      Which novel writers sel- | dom notice;
    The song the blood mosqui- | toes sing,
      And midnight howling of | coyotes.

Although iambic feet predominate in most of the poems, both willful and spontaneous substitutions of various other feet are common, especially anapests (u u l), amphibracs (u l u), and trochées (l u), in that order of relative frequency. What has traditionally been called the "ballad meter" — a line of seven feet with caesura after the fourth — is also very common:

    I just | came down | from Lou- | isville ||
      some pleas- | ures for | to find

Rhyme

ALL OF THE POETRY of this study makes use of rhyme to mark rhythmic groups and the pauses between them. Typically, however, richness of rhyme or rhythm does not divert the reader's attention from narrative, lyrical, or dramatic elements: form is subservient to content and rhymes are rarely distracting. This being the case, rhyme, or what passes for rhyme, encompasses somewhat more than is generally thought. A word is occasionally rhymed with itself. Homonyms are admitted, as are other rhymes with identity not only of the last stressed vowel and all that follows it, but of the preceding consonant as well: *road* / *rode*. A word ending with *s* may be rhymed indiscriminately with words where it does not appear: *sleepers* / *people*. The secondary stress of a multisyllable word is accepted as a rhyme with the stressed syllable of a one-syllable word: *see* / *eternity*. Rhymes are characteristically phonetic, not necessarily visual: in this respect they reflect the peculiarities of "western" pronunciation, be it in genuine folk poems or in pseudo-folk pieces: *out* / *route*; *was* (*wuz*) / *does*. Assonance (i.e., identity of the vowel of the stressed syllable but not of what follows it) is accepted as rhyme: *mind* / *mine*. There is a tolerance of *m* / *n* equivalence. Various other imperfect rhymes are explainable by the fact that perfection of the rhyme is not a primary goal for the creators or the transmitters of folk and primitive poetry. On the other hand, in burlesque-type poems forced rhymes are injected to produce humorous results: *take us* / *Pecos*. Occasionally rhymes are made which willfully bring English and Spanish words into play, or which illuminate facets of the interplay of the Hispanic and Anglo-American cultures: *monotone* / *Conceptión*. Very frequently the images, the place names, the hero images, the peculiarly western human concerns and commitments are illuminated by rhymes which are rare or nonexistent in poetry not indigenous to the American West. The following list is illustrative of this phenomenon, though it is far from complete: *pluck/ chuck*; *nags/bags*; *range/mange*; *ravine/between*; *butte/chute*; *show/Joe/Mexico*; *snow/lasso*; *steed/stampede*; *Tandy/(Rio)*

Grande; O-Bar-O/grow; excuses/cayuses; aim/claim; slicker/ liquor; holts/Colts; fracas/take us/Pecos; part/(Black) Bart; she/Cherokee; cigar/Starr; soon/saloon; hid/Kid; flow/Arapahoe; quick/creek; band/Rio Grande; skin/moccasin; K-M-T/ Santa Fe; coin/Assiniboin; T-Bar-T/scenery; fro/buffalo; ago/ Idaho; Alamo/buffalo/Navajo; spell/corral; freely/Gila (pronounced Hila or Hilee); *fury/Missouri.*

Total lack of rhyme appears sometimes without any visible cause. At other times, however, it has the effect of inviting attention to the rhyme in other stanzas of the poem:

> For the salt lies wide and the salt lies free
> On the dry earth-bed of an ancient sea
> There by the Cimarr*on.*

Refrains and other Repetitive Devices

ALL POETRY, AND EVEN a great deal of literary prose, makes conscious or spontaneous use of repetitive devices. This is especially true of poetry meant to be sung or recited. The poetry studied here forms no exception, though frequency in the use of repetitive devices tends to decrease as the importance of the poem's narrative content increases. In other words, repetitive devices are to be viewed as artistic adumbrations which are rarely essential to the narrative content of the poem. This is not to diminish their importance: they invite attention to significant ideas; they provide a reflective interlude in which there is time to grasp the import of the previous stanza before its successor is offered; they intensify the central thoughts of the poem; they are a vehicle for transition from literal to symbolic or metaphorical meanings; they give the singer a chance to demonstrate his dexterity at "picking" his guitar.

Beyond the formalistic devices noted above there are other

repetitive devices, willed or unconscious, which enrich the effect of this poetry: internal rhyme, parallel construction, the reuse of strong lines having an incremental impact by a slight change therein, refrains either meaningful or nonsensical.

Stanza Form

REGULAR STANZAIC FORM is noted in all but a few of the poems, their structure being marked by rhyme arrangements, by pause (where the poems are read aloud), by spacing or punctuation (where written or printed), and by the conclusion of melodic units (where they are sung). Four-line stanzas rhymed *a a b b* are most common. Rhymed couplets appear also in stanzas of two, six, or eight lines. Refrains or repetitions of the final line in a stanza often intercede between stanzas.

Occasionally octasyllabic quatrains are enriched with internal rhymes which are best examined if we write them using a separate line for each of the internal rhymes occurring regularly therein:

> They seemed to leap
> To meet the sweep
> Of his hands as they flashed in view
> And the cylinders spun
> As they roared as one
> And Denver Dan was through.

Poems of the so-called ballad form (lines of seven metric feet with a caesura after the fourth) appear in stanzas of two, four, six, or eight lines, four being typical.

The Poems

Part One

The Physical and
Human Environment

PART I:

The Physical and Human Environment

1. *Cattle*

In *The Longhorns*, J. Frank Dobie's terse comment on this poem was that ". . . it goes deeper than the map." The author is Berta Hart Nance. (Vaida S. Montgomery, *A Century With Texas Poets and Poetry*. Dallas: Kaleidograph Press, 1934. Pp. 63–64.)

Other states were carved or born,
Texas grew from hide and horn.

Other states are long or wide,
Texas is a shaggy hide,

Dripping blood and crumpled hair;
Some fat giant flung it there—

Laid the head where valleys drain,
Stretched its rump along the plain.

Other soil is full of stones,
Texans plow up cattle-bones.

Herds are buried on the trail,
Underneath the powdered shale;

Herds that stiffened like the snow,
Where the icy northers go.

Other states have built their halls,
Humming tunes along the walls.

Texans watched the mortar stirred,
While they kept the lowing herd.

Stamped on Texan wall and roof
Gleams the sharp and crescent hoof.

High above the hum and stir
Jingle bridle-rein and spur.

Other states were made or born,
Texas grew from hide and horn.

2. On the Arizona Line

A nostalgic piece which captures several of the stereotyped images of the American West: coyote, mountain lion, longhorn, eagle; rim-rock, mesa, purple haze; Indian ruins, aspen groves. (Gordon-Oregon 112: from E. C. Will, Illinois, 1926.)

I am lonesome, oh so lonesome, for the far-away Southwest,
Where the evening shadows lengthen from o'er the mountain crest.
I can hear the night wind sighing through the piñon and the pine,
In the far-off Frisco mountains on the Arizona line.

I can see the sulking coyote through the darkening purple haze,
And I hear the lobo howling down where the longhorns graze.
I can see my campfire flicker, on the rim-rocks shine,
In the far-off Frisco mountains on the Arizona line.

I can see the silvery moonbeams on Dillman's rugged heights,
And I hear the eagle screaming on his swiftly homeward flight.
And somewhere up the cañon I can hear the lion's whine,
In the far-off Frisco mountains on the Arizona line.

I can see the ruined cities of a long forgotten race,
With the ghostly quaking aspen growing round the vacant place.
I can see the darkening shadows on their ancient broken shrine,
In the far-off Frisco mountains on the Arizona line.

I can see Hell-roaring Mesa a-down old Luna way,
Like a lake of molten silver in the moonlight cold and gray,
And I hear the night birds calling from the wild wood tangled vine,
In the far-off Frisco mountains on the Arizona line.

3. *A Prairie Mother's Lullabye*

A lullaby in which western images and sounds are concentrated: to the ever-present mesas and coyotes are added the gray wolf's howl, the lowing of bedded cattle, the rattlesnake, the stunted sage, and especially the songs of the cowboy. The author is said to be E. A. Brininstool. (Hendren 527: newspaper clipping.)

The sunset deepens in the west,
  Faint shadows drift across the sky,
So sleep, dear heart, on mother's breast,
And rock away to dreamy rest,
  To her low soothing lullabye.
The night wind breathes across the plain,
  The moonbeams shed a luster bright
The cattle low a weird refrain,
  Upon the starlit summer night.

REFRAIN:
  By-low, babe, oh rockabye,
  By low, babe, oh hushabye,
Down the winding trail thy Daddy rides where the shadows creep.
  So-ho, baby, close thine eyes,
  By-low, baby, the sunset dies.
Sleep, my little prairie wild flower.

Upon the mesa, bare and brown,
  The slinking coyotes prowl
And, hark, upon the silent air,
In ghostly cadence echoes there
  Floats forth the gray wolf's mournful howl.
The cowboy's song rings loud and clear,
  As round the bedded cattle he rides,
And from the stunted sagebrush near
  The sluggish rattler smoothly glides.

4. *Arizona and New Mexico*

". . . by a soldier who had spent three years of service in the two territories," i.e., Pvt. George Canterbury.

In poignant vein a keen observer and skilled satirist evokes an array of images which might have turned the gentler breed toward more hospitable domains. It didn't. Quite the contrary, the restless and the adventurous rushed headlong into the West to engage its particular brand of malign nature in sinew-to-sinew combat. (J. H. Beadle, *The Undeveloped West: or Five Years in the Territories*. Philadelphia: National Publishing Co., 1873. Pp. 536–40.)

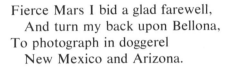

Fierce Mars I bid a glad farewell,
   And turn my back upon Bellona,
To photograph in doggerel
   New Mexico and Arizona.

The stinging grass and thorny plants
   And all its prickly tropic glories,
The thieving, starved inhabitants,
   Who look so picturesque in stories.

The dusty, long, hot, dreary way,
   Where 'neath a blazing sun you totter,
To reach a camp at close of day
   And find it destitute of water.

The dying mule, the dried-up spring,
   Which novel writers seldom notice;
The song the blood mosquitoes sing,
   And midnight howling of coyotes.

Tarantulas and centipedes,
   Horn'd toads and piercing mezquit daggers,
With thorny bushes, grass and weeds,
   To bleed the traveler as he staggers.

Why paint things in a rosy light,
   And never tell the simple fact thus —
How one sits down to rest at night,
   And often squats upon a cactus?

As desert, mountain — rock and sand —
  Comprise the topographic features,
There's little left at my command
  Except to paint the living creatures.

In point of energy and sense,
  The wild Apaches are the head men,
And so, in fairness, I commence
  To tell you something of the red men.

Each mountain chain contains a hive
  Of these marauding sons of thunder,
Who somehow manage and contrive
  To live upon *mescal* and plunder.

            *   *   *

Too long my pen has dwelt upon
  These foes to railroads, soap and labor,
A few short years, and they are gone
  Beyond the reach of prayer or saber.

Now turn we to another race
  Inhabiting this sunny region,
In calm and fearless truth to trace
  Their manners, habits and religion.

There is no fairer law than that
  Which gives to Caesar what is Caesar's,
Yet this is not a land of fat
  Because the people are called "Greasers."

These natives, in a Yankee's eyes,
  Have neither virtue, brains nor vigor —
A most unhappy compromise
  Between the Ingin and the nigger.

Their language is a mongrel whine,
  From which the meaning seems to vanish,
Like strength from lager beer or wine —
  A parody upon the Spanish.

On what they live — besides the air —
  You may perhaps be interested;
They have as queer a bill of fare
  As human stomach e'er digested.

Continued

They eat *frijoles, carne,* corn,
  And on a hog's intestines riot;
Tortillas, sheeps-head (hair and horn),
  With *chile* for the favorite diet.

*   *   *

But little care he ever feels,
  So he but apes the Spanish hero,
With monstrous spurs upon his heels,
  And on his head a broad *sombrero.*

He looks so grim and full of fight,
  You might suppose his temper soured;
But danger turns him nearly white,
  And proves the hero is a coward.

He grimly scowls at *Gringo* jokes,
  Though he has not a single *tlaco,*
With dignity he calmly smokes
  His cigarette of bad tobacco.

Smoking and lolling in the shade,
  Their lazy souls no thought perplexes;
But make a chimney undismayed
  Out of the noses of both sexes.

They tell a thousand barefaced lies,
  To all the saints in heaven appealing,
Confess their sins with tearful eyes,
  Devoutly pray—but keep on stealing.

They go to church, believe in hell,
  (Where their own torment must be hot ones),
They play on fiddles, ring a bell,
  And worship God with drums and shot-guns.

*   *   *

Upon their heads in triumph reign
  Great swarms of vermin, fat and saucy;
Those rovers of the Spanish *mane,*
  Cruise fearless o'er an ocean glossy.

Their mode of travel on the road
  Would frighten one who never met a
Dirty, screaming, stupid load
  Of Greasers in an old *curreta.*

Great wooden wheels, devoid of grease,
  And oxen rushing with a vengeance —
A noise like forty thousand geese,
  Or like a score of new steam-engines.

They plow the soil with forked logs,
  For fuel dig the earth with shovels,
Cut grass with hoes, chain up their hogs,
  And keep their horses in their hovels.

When Gabriel plays his final trump,
  And all the nations are paraded
For grand inspection in a lump,
  This breed will prove the most degraded.

An earthquake which should sink the land,
  Some great subterranean motion,
And leave this tract of barren sand
  The pavement of a heaving ocean,

Some huge convulsive water shake,
  Some terrible spasmodic movement,
Subsiding but to leave a lake,
  Would be a most desired improvement.

I've not, in picturing this clime,
  Been either brilliant or pathetic,
But told of facts in simple rhyme,
  By far more truthful than poetic.

My photograph, I must confess,
  The country does by no means flatter —
The people and their customs less,
  But it is *true* — that's what's the matter.

If any think me too severe,
  Or call my yarn a wicked libel,
I'll take, to prove myself sincere,
  My "davy" on a Mormon Bible.

5. *Someone's Opinion of Arizona*

Ascribed to Charlie Brown, proprietor of the Congress Hall gambling saloon in Tucson in the mid-1800s.

That Satan—astute anticreator—had a hand in shaping the Southwest was no deterrent to men bent upon its submission. Two distinct though interrelated poems deal with this topic: "Someone's Opinion of Arizona," given here, and "Hell in Texas," of which "Alaska, or Hell of the Yukon" (No. 6, following) is an obvious parody: as the very last frontier, Alaska merits inclusion here. (FAC II 434: manuscript, Arizona Historical Library.)

The devil was given permission one day
To select a land for his own special sway,
So he hunted around for a month or more
And fussed and fumed and terribly swore
But at last was delighted a country to view
Where the prickly pear and catclaw grew.
With a brief survey and without further excuse
He selected the land by the Santa Cruz,
He saw there were still improvements to make
For he felt his own reputation at stake.
An idea struck him, he swore by his horns
That he would make a complete vegetation of thorns.
So he studded the land with the prickly pear
And scattered the cacti everywhere,
The Spanish dagger, pointed and tall,
And at last the *cholla* to outstick them all.
He imported the Apache direct from hell
The size of the sweet-scented ranks to swell,
And legions of skunks whose loud, loud smell
Perfumed this bleak country he loved so well.
And for his life he couldn't see why
The river should any more water supply
And he swore if they furnished another drop
You might use his head and horns for a mop.
He sanded the rivers till they were dry
And poisoned them all with alkali
And promised himself on this limey brink
The control of all who should from them drink.

He saw there was still one improvement to make
So imported the scorpion and rattlesnake
That all who came to this country to dwell
Wouldn't fail to imagine a sure enough hell.
He fixed up the heat at one hundred and eleven
And banished forever the moisture of heaven
And said as he heard the hot furnace roar
That the mercury might reach five hundred or more.
After fixing these things so thorny and well
He said, "I'll be damned if this don't beat hell."
Then he spread out his wings and away he flew
And vanished forever in a blaze of blue.
And now, no doubt, in some corner of hell
He gloats over the work he completed so well
And vows Arizona can never be beat
For thorns, tarantulas, snakes, and heat.
For with all his plans carried out so well
He feels well assured Arizona is hell.

6. *Alaska, or Hell of the Yukon*

(PNFQ 2)

The devil in hell we are told was chained,
Thousands of years he there remained.
He did not complain nor did he groan,
But determined to have a hell of his own,
Where he could torment the souls of men
Without being chained in a solitary pen.

Continued

So he asked the Lord if he had any land
In a colder clime than a poor soul could stand.
The Lord said yes, but it's not much use,
It's cold Alaska, and it is cold as the deuce.
In fact, old boy, the place is bare,
I don't think you could make a good hell here.

The devil said he couldn't see why,
For he sure knew his business and would like to try.
So the bargain was made and the deed was given
And the devil quickly departed from heaven.
We next see the devil far up in the north
Examining Alaska, to see what it is worth.

From the top of McKinley he looked at the truck,
And said, "If I get this for nothing I still am stuck."
But, oh, it was fine to be out in the cold.
The wind blew a gale and the devil grew bold,
And there on the height of the mountain he planned
To make of Alaska the home of the damned.

A different place from the old-fashioned hell
Where each soul burned in an awful hot cell.
He used every means that a wise devil needed
To make a good hell, and he sure succeeded.

He filled the air with millions of gnats
And spread the Yukon over the flats,
And set a line of volcanoes in Yawnamice Pass,
And bred mosquitoes in the dungre grass.
And made six months' night where it's sixty below,
A howling wind and a pelting snow;
Six months' day with a spell now and then
Too hot for the devil, too hot for his men;
Hungry dogs and wolves by the pack
That when they yell sends chills down your back.

And when you mush o'er the barren expanse,
The wind blows wicked holes in your pants.
But of all the pests the imps could devise,
The Yukon mosquitoes were the devil's pride.
They're like the rattlesnake's bite or scorpion's sting,
And they measure six inches from wing to wing.

And the devil said when he fashioned these,
"Each one will be worth a million fleas."
And over the mountains, valleys and plains,
Where the dew falls heavy and sometimes rains,
He grew a few flowers and berries, just for a bluff,
For the devil sure knew how to peddle his stuff.
To show how well he knew his game,
The devil next salted his new hell claim,
Put gold nuggets in some of his streams
To lure men on in their hopes and dreams.
He hid them deep in the glacial ice
Like a reformed city hides its vice.
He bid Dame Rumor to spread the news
To all the world and its holy crews
That there was gold in heaps and piles
In all the colors and all the styles.
He grinned a grin, a satisfied grin,
And said, "Now watch the fools rush in.
They will fight for gold and steal and slay,
But in the end it's me they will pay."
Oh, what a fine hell this that the devil owns
His trails are marked by frozen bones;
The wild wind moans o'er plain, hill and dell,
It's a hell of a place he has his hell.
Now you know, should anyone ask you,
What kind of a place is our own Alaska.

7. *On the Frisco River*

Topography, vegetation, and animal life all act like so many drugs or malevolent spirits upon men who sense that resistance is futile. Our one and only encounter with this poem is a copy sent by N. Howard (Jack) Thorp to the New Mexico files of the W.P.A. Writers Project in the Library of Congress. (FAC II 92.)

The snow clung cold to the northern slope
The Frisco coiled like a silver rope;
And hot on the scrub and the cactus gray
The level rays of the March sun lay.

From up the fire of the freighter's camp
Unquenched by the chill of the valley damp
The sweet dense smoke of the juniper wood
Rose up like joss to the great god good.

A bald-faced steer, sides lank and thin,
Looked up from the mesquite with a yellow grin;
While on the arm of a stunted oak
A dingy buzzard the silence broke.

For it's the land of *frijoles* and sin,
Where men ride fast and ponies are thin.
Yet all who tarry within this land
Are held there tight by an iron hand.

Mañana, they say, they'll hit the trail
That leads from cactus to where the mail
Comes in each day, and life throbs hard—
The land of the movies and the playing card.

But still they stay while life rolls by
And on the Frisco they'll surely die;
There, graves are deep 'neath boulders gray,
To keep the roving coyotes at bay.

8. *On Salt Plains*

Malign nature and enraged Indians give no quarter whatsoever to two unfortunate teamsters, result: a prairie burial. The author is Daisy Lemon Coldiron. (*Ballads of the Plains*. Dallas: Kaleidograph Press, 1950. P. 24. Reproduced by permission of Kara Lee Eikleberry.)

> Go gather a load of the white, white salt
>   (Two cowboys all alone)
> For the salt lies wide and the salt lies free
> On the dry earth-bed of an ancient sea
>   There by the Cimarron.
> O is it the salt in your eyes, poor boys,
>   (For the wild winds blow and blow)
> Or is it salt *tears* in your eyes, poor boys —
>   Not tears for you could not know!
>
> The cattle herds wait for the white, white salt —
>   (Two mothers wait for their boys)
> Your shovel and spade will dig a lone grave
> In the dry joint clay where wire grasses wave
>   While the sailing buzzards poise.
> O the flint-sharp darts in your hearts, brave hearts,
>   Four arrows in poor Bristow's,
> In Fred Clark's body four more so sharp,
>   And the long wind blows and blows!
>
> O who was to warn you, who was to tell —
>   (Your wagon wheels, did they moan?)
> Dull Knife and his band have escaped from the Fort
> But there is no messenger bearing report
>   To you, two teamsters alone!
> Comrades ease you down in the clay, red clay
>   (Where the crisping wire grass grows)
> Praying "God, take care of these two poor boys!"
>   While the strong wind blows and blows!

9. Geronimo

The storied Apache chief is viewed with fear, awe, and admiration. Written by Ernest McGaffey. (Edmund Clarence Stedman, *An American Anthology, 1787–1900.* Boston: Houghton, Mifflin Co., 1900. P. 670.)

Beside that tent and under guard in majesty alone he stands,
As some chained eagle, broken-winged, with eyes that gleam like
      smouldering brands, —
A savage face, streaked o'er with paint, and coal-black hair in
      unkempt mane,
Thin, cruel lips, set rigidly, — a red Apache Tamerlane.

As restless as the desert winds, yet here he stands like carven stone,
His raven locks by breezes moved, and backward o'er his
      shoulders blown;
Silent, yet watchful as he waits, robed in his strange, barbaric guise,
While here and there go searchingly the cat-like wanderings
      of his eyes.

The eagle feather on his head is dull with many a bloody stain,
While darkly on his lowering brow forever rests the mark of Cain.
Have you but seen a tiger caged and sullen through his
      barriers glare?
Mark well his human prototype, the fierce Apache fettered there.

10. *Indian Legend of the Canyon*

A whole generation of Americans pulsed with wonder at the reading, recitation, or memorization of this synthetic and highly literate legend of the Colorado River Canyon, said to have been written by Jeremiah Mahoney and published in *Barnes Fifth Reader,* 1884. The Indian is noble, idealized even by the Anglo-American, but only from the moment that he is no longer a threat. (PNFQ 219.)

Where the sunset's golden gleamings
    On the rocky highlands rest,
'Neath the moonlight's silver beamings
    Of the distant dreamy West,
Once there roamed an Indian lover,
    With his fawn-eyed Indian fair —
Lover blithe as mountain rover,
    Maiden rich in flowing hair.

But the sleep that knows no waking
    Chilled the gentle maiden's breast,
And the Brave, all hope forsaking,
    Laid her in the hill to rest.
Laid her where the eye may wander
    Far o'er slopes and ledges steep,
And the mind on billows ponder,
    Billows grand but locked in sleep.

Then the Brave's bold eye was darkened,
    And his hand forgot the bow,
Naught to human speech he harkened,
    Naught but sorrow would he know.
Frozen was his heart of gladness
    As the summits capped with snow.
Dark his soul with sullen sadness
    As their cavern depths below.

But the Great Good Spirit sought him,
    Sought him in his speechless grief,
And in kindly promise brought him
    Matchless comfort and relief.
"Come," he said, "and see thy dearest,
    See her in her spirit home,
Towards the Southland, 'tis the nearest,
    We shall journey, hither come."

Continued

And they went—the Spirit leading—
    Speeding with unmeasured force,
Neither hill nor valley heeding,
    On, straight onward, was their course.
With the whirlwind's footstep striding,
    By the smooth and rock-cut ledge,
Hills with earthquake's plow dividing,
    Ploughshare sharp as lightning's edge.

Such their way through hill and valley,
    Cold and narrow, dark and steep,
Opened the rock-embosomed alley,
    Cut a thousand fathoms deep.
Carving, piercing, cutting thorough,
    Toward the drowsy southern shore,
The Spirit formed the mystic furrow,
    And told its sides to meet no more.

But the Spirit good, all knowing,
    Feared lest men's unresting race,
By the mystic pathway going,
    Should mar the Spirit hunter's chase.
'Twas then he gave the torrents headway,
    A thousand, thousand streams were poured.
'Twas then adown its narrow bedway
    That first the Colorado roared.

And still the diamond drops are speeding,
    Down a million rippling rills,
The headlong, rushing cascades feeding
    From liquid hoard of snow-clad hills.
And still the voices of the river
    Within the canyon's depths are heard,
In echoing sounds to speak forever
    At the bidding of His word.

11. *Dust or Bust*

This is the kind of tale you might have gotten straight off the cuff from the puncher whose foot was next to yours on the rail at the bar—a tale about a tough but not-too-bright *hombre* who pushed his luck once too often and got his due. (PNFQ 121.)

Bandanna Jack was in Mexico
  An' stayin' there for his health,
But he got in a game with Six-Card Joe
  Who coppered Bandanna's wealth.

So Bandanna started north once more,
  To try for another stack,
An' he picked on a bank in Salvador,
  To git him his lost stake back.

He managed the job as a one-man show
  With a gun at the cashier's head,
Who handled the money 'way too slow;
  So Bandanna left him dead.

A posse trailed him for nigh a week,
  But he lost them without a fight.
Then he reached an arroyo near Sandy Creek
  And holed up there all night.

After shiftin' an' cinchin' the money load,
  He rode his pinto down,
For more than a mile on the dusty road,
  To the quiet mining town.

Jack hadn't been eatin' for quite a spell,
  While the posse was on his track,
So he piled in grub at the Grand Hotel,
  An' fed his hoss at the back.

When he comes to pay for the grub an' feed,
  He was feelin' as if he'd bust,
But there on the boss's desk he seed
  A good-sized bag of dust.

Continued

51

He shoots the boss, an' he grabs the bag,
   An' he gallops away from the camp.
He forgits that he's ridin' a worn-out nag,
   Till it drops right down with a cramp.

He packs himself with the gold an' gun
   An' starts on foot with the load,
He travels along, half walk, half run,
   Then the posse comes up the road.

They meet him there in the rocks an' sand
   With a shower of red-hot lead,
An' the gold bags slip from Bandanna's hand,
   As he sinks by a sandhill — dead.

12. Billy the Kid

The several ballads which have circulated in popular tradition concerning Billy the Kid treat him as an unredeemed criminal (as does the one given here); as an underdog gone wrong and hence deserving of pity; or else as a hero in full possession of most of the virtues ascribed to cowboys and to westerners generally. See also "Pizen Pete's Mistake," No. 22 of this collection. (Gordon-Oregon 130: from E. C. Will, Murphysboro, Illinois, 1926.)

Billy was a bad man and carried a big gun,
He was always after greasers and kept 'em on the run.

He shot one every morning for to make his morning meal,
And let a white man sass him, he was sure to feel his steel.

He kept folks in hot water and he stole from many a stage,
And when he was full of liquor he was always in a rage.

But one day he met a man who was a whole lot badder,
And now he's dead and we ain't none the sadder.

13. *The Two-Gun Man*

Here the western outlaw is cast as a mythical type whose immortality
is achieved through the persistence of his image in the minds of men.
(Hendren 11: manuscript.)

The two-gun man walked through the town
    And found the sidewalk clear,
He looked around with ugly frown
    But not a soul was near.
The streets were silent, hushed, and still
    No cowboy raised a shout;
Like a panther bent upon the kill
    The two-gun man walked about.

The two-gun man was small and quick,
    His eyes were narrow slits,
He didn't hail from Bitter Creek
    Nor shoot the town to bits.
He drank alone deep drafts of gin,
    Then pushed away his glass,
And silent was each dance hall's din
    When by the door he'd pass.

One day rode forth this man of wrath
    Upon the distant plain
And ne'er did he retrace his path—
    Nor was he seen again.
The cow-town fell into decay,
    No spurred heel pressed its walks,
But through its grass-grown ways they say
    The two-gun man still stalks.

14. *Outlaw Epitaphs*

In the cowboy era realism and honesty seem to have prevailed in epitaphs, or at least those for the graves of men who lived by horse and gun. (FAC II 35: Arizona files, WPA Writers Project, Library of Congress, 1936.)

a. *Billy Grounds*
   This is the grave of Billy Grounds,
   He didn't weigh more'n ninety pounds;
   He was just a kid, as the story goes,
   He sometimes dressed in women's clothes.

   At least, we think this body's him,
   After the shootin' this face was dim;
   It's about his size and about his build,
   And if we ain't got Bill, the devil will.

b. *Minor Owens*
   He lived through an age when the gun was the law,
   And none could beat this man on the draw,
   In Supai Canyon the desert got 'im,
   But Minor Owens is not forgotten.

c. *Jim Genung*
   This is the spot where a gent named Genung,
   Paid with his life for his crimes and his fun,
   At last the law this jasper outwitted,
   He was hung for all the crimes he committed.

d. *Four Texas Train Robbers*
   Four Texas train robbers are buried here,
   No one knows what their names were,
   Two Texas Rangers and a posse from town
   Came out one night and mowed them all down,
   They are buried here, just as they fell,
   We hope their souls are not all in hell!

Continued

e. *Three Fingered Black Jack*

Three fingered Black Jack! Now he was a gent,
With murder in his eye and a soul hell-bent!
He met his death in a canyon pass,
It took fifty men to get him at last.

f. *The Fancy Kid*

Here's where Louis, the Fancy Kid,
Paid a just price for the crimes that he did,
The last one he killed was LULU the doll,
She was a singer, and she was his moll,
He stole from the old and murdered the young,
Then met his death at the muzzle of a gun.

15. *Laramie Trail*

Unlike most other representatives of the law, the troopers who manned the frontier outposts of the West are treated with respect. This is no doubt because their violence was directed not against Anglo-Americans, but against the Indians. Here they loom as an advance party of the new culture. Joseph Mills Hanson is the author. (*Frontier Ballads.* Chicago: A. C. McClurg and Co., 1910. Pp. 40–41.)

Across the crests of the naked hills,
    Smooth-swept by the winds of God,
It cleaves its way like a shaft of gray,
    Close-bound by the prairie sod.
It stretches flat from the sluggish Platte
    To the lands of forest shade;
The clean trail, the lean trail,
    The trail the troopers made.

It draws aside with a wary curve
    From the lurking, dark ravine,
It launches fair as a lance in air
    O'er the raw-ribbed ridge between;
With never a wait it plunges straight
    Through river or reed-grown brook;
The deep trail, the steep trail,
    The trail the squadrons took.

They carved it well, those men of old,
    Stern lords of the border war,
They wrought it out with their sabres stout
    And marked it with their gore.
They made it stand as an iron band
    Along the wild frontier;
The strong trail, the long trail,
    The trail of force and fear.

For the stirring note of the bugle's throat
    Ye may hark to-day in vain,
For the track is scarred by the gang-plow's shard
    And gulfed in the growing grain.
But wait to-night for the moonrise white;
    Perchance ye may see them tread
The lost trail, the ghost trail,
    The trail of the gallant dead.

Continued   57

'Twixt cloud and cloud o'er the pallid moon
  From the nether dark they glide
And the grasses sigh as they rustle by
  Their phantom steeds astride.
By four and four as they rode of yore
  And well they know the way;
The dim trail, the grim trail,
  The trail of toil and fray.

With tattered guidons spectral thin
  Above their swaying ranks,
With carbines swung and sabres slung
  And the gray dust on their flanks.
They march again as they marched it then
  When the red men dogged their track,
The gloom trail, the doom trail,
  The trail they came not back.

They pass, like a flutter of drifting fog,
  As the hostile tribes have passed,
As the wild-wing'd birds and the bison herds
  And the unfenced prairies vast,
And those who gain by their strife and pain
  Forget, in the land they won,
The red trail, the dead trail,
  The trail of duty done.

But to him who loves heroic deeds
  The far-flung path still bides,
The bullet sings and the war-whoop rings
  And the stalwart trooper rides.
For they were the sort from Snelling Fort
  Who traveled fearlessly
The bold trail, the old trail,
  The trail to Laramie.

16. *When I Am a Millionaire.*

In this poem an over-burden of humor comes close to concealing the bittersweet of its real substance: the "golden pipe dream" of the next-to-last line ignites, like dynamite, all the heartbreaks of a frustrated life. It is said to have been written by J. C. Crowell in 1913. (JL 497.)

I am going out to Nevada, but not there for my health,
I am going out to rustle and get my share of wealth,
And when I've made my little pile, oh, I'll not linger there,
I'll tell you what I am going to do when I am a millionaire.

I'll have a golden railway built upon a golden track
And tie it down with a golden chain in case I should come back.
I'll have a golden house and lot, also a golden stair,
I'll be a golden son of a bitch when I am a millionaire.

I'll have a golden wedding upon a golden summer's day,
Out among the wheat fields and the new mown hay.
I'll have goldfish for my breakfast, and gold dust in my hair,
I'll have more money than old Jay Gould when I am a millionaire.

I'll buy me five years' room rent and a thousand pounds of dope,
I'll buy me a golden pipe and then proceed to smoke.
While lying on my golden couch, build castles in the air,
I'll have a golden pipe dream — yes — when I am a millionaire.

17. *The Wolf Mountain Stampede*

A bit of western realism (with overtones of pathos) concerning the fevers and chills of prospecting. (Hendren 220: manuscript.)

This is the man of whom we read
Who left Deadwood on the big stampede
He's now returned all tattered and torn
From looking for gold out on the Big Horn.
  He has no malt, he has no cat,
  He has no coat, he has no hat.

His trousers are patched with an old flour sack
With "For Family Use" to be seen on the back.
His beard is shaggy, his hair is long,
And this is the burden of his song:
  "If ever I hear, if ever I read
  Of ary another Great Stampede
  I'll listen but I'll give no heed
  But stay in my cabin in Deadwood."

He paid ten dollars the other day
For a mule to carry his grub away
He packed his grub in half an hour:
Two gallons of whisky, one pound of flour.

He bought a shovel and borrowed a pick,
He spotted his watch and went on tick
For a side of bacon and a can of lard.
Now look at his fate! My, isn't it hard?

He walked all day and most of the night
And now he is back, a sorrowful sight
To the cabin he built in Deadwood.

18. *The Ballad of Tonopah Bill*

This roughhewn prospector's ballad merits, and indeed demands, some soul-probing: discovery of the pathos of a compulsion so great that humans will stampede out of heaven into hell itself on the mere rumor of a gold strike—the perpetrator falling victim to his own lie! (Hendren 4: manuscript.)

Tonopah Bill was a desert rat who had traveled the gold
      camps through;
He was first to hear of the latest strike wherever the rumors flew.
In the frozen north or the Rio Grande he had looked for
      elusive pay,
And the tales of his wonderful luck would spread in a most
      remarkable way.

He talked in an optimistic vein, as fitted the mining game,
And he carried his art to the Other Side when he staked his
      final claim,
For he started forth in the Milky Way and he rapped on the
      pearly gates,
And when St. Peter confronted him he asked for permanent rates.

But the good Saint shook his head and said, "No place in here
      for you!
We want no more within our door of the lawless mining crew.
They are blasting the golden streets at night to search for the
      hidden vein,
With hammer and drill and a double shift they prospect a
      copper stain.

"They have pitched their tents and staked their claims as far as
      the eye can see,
For they cannot forget the lure of the gold in all eternity."
Now Tonopah Bill grinned a knowing grin and spoke in a
      forceful way,
"Good Saint," quoth he, "there's a trick or two on that gang
      I would like to play.

Continued

"With a word or two I will send them hence and peace once
     more will reign.
They will pass at night through the pearly gates and never
     return again."
It sounded remarkably like a bluff but the need of the Saint
     was sore,
And Bill had a confident way with him, as I have remarked before.

So the gates flew wide and he entered in, and straight to the
     camp he drew,
Where he told a marvelous tale to that restless mining crew.
No thought they gave that the tale was wild, no time did they
     take to prove,
But straight as the news was flashed around the camp was
     on the move.

St. Peter looked in a vast amaze and, "Tell me," he began,
"What means you used to start so quick this mining caravan."
"I told them news of a strike," said Bill, "that just was
     made Below.
A million dollars it ran to the ton, and plenty there to show.

"Free milling rock in a fissure vein, well worth a heavy bet,
And I said if they hurried up a bit some ground was open yet."
The good Saint looked aghast and said, "This story is absurd."
"Perhaps," said Bill with a cheerful grin. "'Tis a rumor that
     I heard."

It was not long ere the watchful Saint saw Bill approach again,
His mining tools were on his back and argument was in vain.
"I am mighty sorry to go," said he, "and to say good bye to you,
But I'm off to join the others, for the rumor might be true."

19. *Western Justice*

Judges and justices of the peace are typically treated either as inhuman beings or as hyper-westerners who mete out justice in the same rough-shod way a cowboy assails a critter. This item is attributed to Arthur L. Rafter. (Hendren 189: manuscript.)

Yuh don't see any judges settin' on the bench today
Like ol' Judge White—who used to set out Colorado way:

A dirty squaw man, Cockney Tom, a measley thieving skunk,
Drifts into Badger Bill's saloon a startin' his weekly drunk.
He's pickin' a fight with Dandy Jim an' talkin' o' slinging lead,
When, somehow or other, Jim's gun explodes an' Cockney Tom
    drops dead.

Wa'al old Judge White—he hears the case 'til 'long 'bout
    dinner time,
Then he up and says to Dandy Jim, "This shootin' is a crime.
I got the peace an' welfare o' the county to consider,
So now I'm going to sentence yuh to apolergize to the widder."

A slick haired stranger from the east sneaks out o' town one day,
After beatin' ol' man Murray bad, an' takin' his hoss away.
A sheriff's posse hits the trail an' brings him back that night,
Next morning they yanks him into court an' he's tried by old
    Judge White.

When the Judge says, "Guilty. String him up," the stranger
    starts to squeal.
"Yuh can't hang me for that," he says. "Your honor, I appeal."
Judge White says very solemn like, "Wa'al, if wust comes to wust
I'll have ter grant thet thar appeal, but I'm going to hang
    you fust."

Thar ain't no real good judge sittin' on the bench today
Like ol' Judge White, who used to sit out Colorado way.

20. *The Law West of the Pecos*

Roy Bean is a willfully humorous caricature of the first generation of
justices of the peace in the West: three or four ballads about this in-
imitable westerner have been sung throughout the West and have been
published many times. This one is by S. Omar Barker. (*Rawhide
Rhymes*. Garden City, N.Y.: Doubleday and Co., p. 45. Copyright
1968 by S. Omar Barker.)

Judge Roy Bean of Vinegarroon
Held high court in his own saloon.
For a killin', a thievin' or other such fracas,
Bean was the law out west of the Pecos.
Set on a keg and allowed no foolin'.
Closed every case with "That's my rulin'!"
A gun-butt thump and a judgey snort
Announced to the boys he was openin' court;
And every once in a while or less,
He'd thump with his gun for a short recess,
Step to the bar like a sly old lynx
And call all present to buy some drinks.
Juryman, witness, thirsty or dry,
Stepped right up for their ol' red-eye.

Once on a jury a man called Hanks
Set where he was and says "No thanks!"
"Now, by gobs," was Judge Bean's snort,
"I fine you ten for contempt of court!"
Hanks, he hemmed and Hanks, he hawed,
But finally out of his pants he drawed
A bill for twenty and paid his fine.
"Ten bucks change," he says, "is mine."
"Change?" roars the Law of the Pecos Range.
"This here court don't make no change!"
Judge Bean smiled his six-gun smile:
"I raise you ten and take your pile!
Now, by gobs, gents, without no foolin',
Wet up your whistles, for that's my rulin'!"

Oh, out in the West when the range was raw,
West of the Pecos *law was law*!

64

21. *Root, Hog, or Die*

The plight of the tenderfoot on the frontier was nearly always a sad one. Men already acclimated to the new environment took delight in making the "outsider's" experience as uncomfortable as they could, as in this song which has been refurbished or parodied scores of times to meet the needs of most of the Anglo-American's pioneering experiences, from the Tea Party to the present. (Hendren 488: newspaper clipping.)

I left old Indiana in the year of eighty-two,
And when I got to Kansas I was feeling rather blue;
I hadn't a cent of money a meal's victuals to buy,
The only thing for me to do was root, hog, or die.

My kinsfolks all asked me and begged me not to roam
And wander into Kansas, so far away from home;
I think of what my sister said when she bade me goodby,
When I left old Indiana to root, hog, or die.

I went out in the country and went to making hay,
The wages that I got was a dollar and a half a day;
I had cold supper every night, but there was no use to cry,
The only thing for me to do was root, hog, or die.

I went to Kansas City and stayed a day or two,
'Twas there I met some strangers who helped to put me through;
'Twas a nice game of poker, they handled the cards so shy,
They soon got all my money, and said, "Root, hog, or die."

This made me very angry and I began to swear,
I swallowed down the corn juice till I got on a tear;
The marshall of the city, who happened to be standing by,
He took me to the calaboose to root, hog, or die.

They took me to the courtroom next morning just at ten,
There sat the judge and a dozen other men;
They fined me twenty dollars, which I thought was very high,
But it was no use of kicking, it was root, hog, or die.

Continued

Then just as I was beginning to repent,
My fine was twenty dollars and I didn't have a cent,
As good luck would have it, a friend was standing by
He paid that twenty dollars and said, "Root, hog, or die."

Come all you jolly young fellows, pray take my advice,
Never play poker, or go shaking dice,
For if you do, you'll get too much old rye,
And they'll land you in the cooler to root, hog, or die.

22. *Pizen Pete's Mistake*

A classical barroom interchange between two gunmen, a bully and an underdog. The outcome is inevitable. The stuff of which this poem is made has been among the hard goods of the western movies since they began. Said to have been written by Merrill Honey. (Hendren 532: newspaper clipping.)

It was in the Yellow Dog Saloon one sultry summer night,
Old "Pizen Pete" was on the prod and looking for a fight.
With a forty-five in either hand, red whiskers and long hair,
'Twas enough to make a man turn pale to see him standing there.

And then there came into the room, as the swinging doors
    swung wide,
A young lad of scarce twenty years, with a gun on either side.
He did not look to right or left as he walked up to the bar,
And leaning there he calmly said, "A big drink of Three Star."

He raised the whiskey to his lips; Pizen Pete stepped back
    with a sneer;
His six-gun roared and, as it did, the glass seemed to disappear.
The stranger slowly turned around, and I saw his face turn red.
"Do that again, old timer, and I'll burn yuh down!" he said.

"Go ahead and draw," said Pete, with a grin. His own gun was
    in hand.
"Just make a move for your six-gun, an' I'll kill yuh where
    yuh stand!"
The youngster quickly jumped aside, and his guns began to roar,
And when the smoke had cleared away, Pizen Pete lay on the floor.

"Say, stranger, what's your name?" I asked. "It seems like I've
    seen your face."
He didn't turn or answer, but quickly left the place.
He went out and mounted his pony; I heard him as he did,
And then his voice came drifting back: "My name is Billy the Kid."

Part Two

The Cowboy and
Other Western Types

PART II

The Cowboy and Other Western Types

23. *The Cowboy*

Already in the early 1880s the mythical cowboy type was beginning to emerge: footloose, man of muscular action, carouser, gunman — and admirable still. (*Kansas Cowboy,* Dodge City, November 8, 1884.)

> What is it has no fixed abode
> Who seeks adventures by the load —
> An errant knight without a code?
> > The cowboy.
>
> Who finds it pleasure cows to punch
> When he would a whole herd bunch —
> Who ready for a fine grass lunch?
> > The cowboy.
>
> Who is it paints the town so red
> And in the morning has a head
> Upon him like a feather bed?
> > The cowboy.
>
> Who is it with unbounded skill
> Will shoot big bullets with a will
> That generally has the effect to kill?
> > The cowboy.
>
> Who is it, after all, who makes
> Town trade good and uniformly takes
> For big hearts what is called "the cake"?
> > The cowboy.

24. The Cowboy's Wishes

D. J. White, a puncher in the 1880s, wrote this satirical piece on observing "city" cowboys seeking employment at the occasion of a stockgrower's meeting. How ironical it is that White's caricature should resemble so much the yet-to-evolve image of the movie cowboy! (*Stockgrowers Journal,* Miles City, Montana, April 7, 1894.)

I want to be a cowboy and with the cowboys stand,
With leather chaps upon me and a six gun in my hand.
And, while the foreman sees me, I'll make some winter plays*
But I will catch a regular when the herd's thrown out to graze.

I'll have a full-stamped saddle and silver mounted bit
With conchas big as dollars and silvered spurs, to wit.
With a long rawhide reata and a big Colt forty-five.
I'll be a model puncher as sure as you're alive.

I want to be a tough man, and be so very bad,
With my big white sombrero I'll make the dude look sad.
I'll get plumb full of bug juice and shoot up the whole town,
When I start out to have a time you bet I'll do it brown.

I want to be a buster and ride the bucking horse
And scratch him in the shoulder, with my silvered spurs, of course.
I'll rake him up and down the side, you bet I'll fan the breeze,
I'll ride him with slick saddle and do it with great ease.

I want to be a top man and work on the outside
So I can ride within the herd and cut it high and wide.
Oh, a rep is what I want to be, and a rep, you bet, I'll make
At punching cows I know I'll shine; I'm sure I'll take the cake.

---

*This seems to mean working in a manner which would cause the boss to keep him employed throughout the year: i.e., a "regular" job.

25. *Cowboy*

The all-American boy of the era of competitive sports has his antecedents in this turn-of-the-century cowboy who is honest, sun-hardened, unbroken, tough—the type many Americans would love to put in the White House. The author is said to be John Antrobus. (Gordon-Oregon 129: from E. C. Will, Illinois, 1926.)

Great is your heart, your big brave heart,
   Cowboy.
Good and raw and bold and wide,
Fit to match your honest hide,
And every beat is clean inside,
   Cowboy.

Clear is the sheen of your untamed eye,
   Cowboy.
A little bit of your unmasked sky,
With nothing slick or smooth or sly,
But altogether, a damn good eye,
   Cowboy.

Where did you really come from, son?
   Cowboy.
You outlaw, unbroke son-of-a-gun,
Handy with your feet, but bad on the run
Once you know a scrap's begun,
   Cowboy.

What will you do when the round-up's done?
   Cowboy.
Where will you be when they ring the bell?
And where are the tales you then will tell?
Will you fight broncs on the range of Hell?
   Cowboy.

I like the cut of your sun-cooked jaw,
   Cowboy.
And doff my hat to your code and law
You're the whitest man I ever saw,
And I'm plumb delighted to shake your paw,
   Cowboy.

26. *Dakota, the Beauty of the West*

This poem strongly indicates that what the western settlers were leaving behind deserved being left, and what they found was what they were looking for. (PNFQ 20.)

From Illinois I started a location for to find,
I heard of a distant country, a country most sublime,
A land of milk and honey and waters of the best,
'Twas the state of South Dakota, the Beauty of the West.

I landed in Sioux City, I didn't like the town,
The streets they were so narrow, and muddy was the ground.
I went into a restaurant and wrote upon my chest:
"I'm bound for South Dakota, the Beauty of the West."

Then next I boarded a steamer, "The Northern Belle" by name,
She pulled up her anchor and we were off again.
They rang the bells for Yankton, 'twas there we landed next,
For it was in South Dakota, the Beauty of the West.

The Yankton girls are jolly, the Yankton girls are kind,
I soon forgot poor Polly, the girl I left behind.
For girls of wit and beauty and tempers of the best
Are the girls of South Dakota, the Beauty of the West.

I had not long recruited, not more than a week or two,
I traveled South Dakota, I traveled through and through,
I went into a restaurant and was there a welcome guest,
For I was in South Dakota, the Beauty of the West.

Some folks they call us "Coyotes," but that we do not mind,
We are just as good as Badgers or any other kind,
The "Coyote" girls are cunning, the "Coyote" girls are shy,
I'll marry me a Coyote girl or a bachelor I will die.

I'll wear a stand-up collar, support a handsome wife,
And live in South Dakota the balance of my life.

74

27. *Ranch at Twilight*

Sounds, forms, and scents that mark the West are concentrated here
in such a provocative way as to make the emergence of dude ranches
almost inevitable: otherwise said, myth has created economic enter-
prises. (Hendren 491: newspaper clipping.)

The soothing sigh of the night wind, the whine of a coyote's call,
The lonesome bawl of a maverick, a hush as the shadows fall.

A gleam of light from the ranch house, the smell of food from
      the door,
The laughter of men well contented, the clink of their spurs on
      the floor.

The cool, sweet smell of the prairie, the twang of a cowboy's guitar,
The deep, gleaming blue of the heavens with its brand of a
      silver star.

Saddles hung over the gate-posts, dusty boots lining the wall,
Rest for the hard-riding waddies, peace and contentment for all!

28. *The High Loping Cowboy (Wild Buckeroo)*

This roughhewn bit of doggerel exposes in a candid—if not crude—
way a whole bundle of cowboy and western tags: action and the wander-
lust; the bleak southwestern terrain and its inhospitable fauna and
foliage; Indians, Mexicans, "woman troubles," and weapons; rugged
individuality and chip-on-shoulder human relations. It was written by
Curley W. Fletcher. (*Songs of the Sage.* Los Angeles: Frontier Pub-
lishing Co., 1931. Pp. 68–69.)

I been ridin' fer cattle the most of my life.
I ain't got no family, I ain't got no wife,
I ain't got no kith, I ain't got no kin,
I allus will finish what ere I begin.
I rode down in Texas where the cowboys are tall,
The State's pretty big but the hosses er small.
Fer singin' to cattle, I'm hard to outdo;
I'm a high-lopin cowboy, an' a wild buckeroo.

I rode in Montana an' in Idaho;
I rode for Terasus in old Mexico.
I rope mountain lion an' grizzly bear,
I use cholla cactus fer combin' my hair.
I cross the dry desert, no water between,
I rode through Death Valley without no canteen.
At ridin' dry deserts I'm hard to outdo;
I'm a high-lopin cowboy an' a wild buckeroo.

Why, I kin talk Spanish and Injun to boot,
I pack me a knife and a pistol to shoot.
I got no Señorita, an' I got no squaw,
I got no sweetheart, ner mother-in-law.
I never been tied to no apron strings,
I ain't no devil, but I got no wings.
At uh dodgin' the ladies, I'm hard to outdo;
I'm a high-lopin' cowboy, an' a wild buckeroo.

I drink red whiskey, an' I don't like beer,
I don't like mutton, but I do like steer.
I will let you alone if you leave me be,
But don't you get tough an' crawl on me.
I'll fight you now at the drop of a hat,
You'll think you're sacked up with a scratchin' wild cat.
At rough ready mixin' I'm hard to outdo;
I'm a high-lopin' cowboy, an' a wild buckeroo.

29. *Ranch Life, or Idyl of the Plains*

The mythical cowboy image was not born full blown. The earliest attempts to portray him gave him more brawn than brain, more sheer cussedness than judgment. (*Kansas Cowboy,* Dodge City, June 28, 1884.)

A man there lives on the Western plain,
With a ton of fight and an ounce of brain,
Who herds the cattle and rides the train
    And goes by the name of cowboy.

He shoots with pistol and carves with knife,
He feels unwell unless in strife,
He laughs at death and mocks at life,
    For he is the terrible cowboy.

He snuffs out candles with pistol balls,
He snuffs out lives in drunken brawls,
He gets snuffed out in gambling halls,
    This wayward, frolicsome cowboy.

He riots in cities and towns and browbeats,
He drives policemen off the streets,
He fills with terror all he meets,
    For all give way to the cowboy.

Ten cowboys drunk near a small station,
Ten pistols ring in sepulchral tune,
Ten corpses stare at the big white moon,
    And where, oh, where is the cowboy?

30. *Braggin' Bill's Fortytude*

In tall tales, especially versified ones, there is more art than meets the eye. The structure is as balanced as a sentence out of Cicero, and the language comes straight from the range despite flawless rhythm and rhyme. Authorship is ascribed to C. Wiles Hallock. (Hendren 188: manuscript.)

The days of yore—both good and ill
Was happy days for Braggin' Bill.

"In former times," said Bill, "a man
Jest had to be more subtile than
The sissified and sickly jays
Of these plumb tame, downtrodden days.
In sixty-nine," says he, "when I
Was young, adventuresome and spry
A feller had to be possess't
Of marv'lous fortytude out West,

"In sixty-nine or there about
When I was but a simple lout
I ran nine hundred steers—alone—
To Denver up from San Antone.
'Twas in the winter that I went
With that shebang of discontent
Through deserts bleak and blizzards bitter
And never lost a single critter.

"One night when I was thus engaged
While tempest howled and blizzard raged
A bothersome event occurred,
A thousand wolves attacked the herd.
But such a grim emergency
Was not a thing to baffle me,
Them days a feller was prepared
For such events, I wasn't scared.

Continued

"With courage modern herders lack
I charged into that savage pack
A flingin' snowballs left and right
At them fierce critters with all my might.
The blizzard raged so frigid thick
It wasn't hard to do the trick,
I ketched the snow a swirlin' round
Before it ever tetched the ground,

"And fashioned into balls them flakes
As hard as rocks—for goodness sakes—
And flung 'em with such deadly aim
I slew a thousand wolves with same,
And saved them critters' every gizzard
From ravin' beasts and ragin' blizzard,
Which wasn't toilsome, glory be,
For such a cunny coot as me."

No saddle yaps, I know, could fill
The noble boots of Braggin' Bill.

31. *A Texas Idyl*

The tradition for creative bragging, in prose or in verse, goes back to colonial times. Three cowboy examples follow. (*The Kansas Cowboy,* Dodge City, July 12, 1884.)

I'm a buzzard from the Brazos on a tear,
    Hear me toot,
I'm a lifter of the flowing locks of hair,
    Hear me toot,
I'm a racker from the Rockies
And all of the town the talk is
"He's a pirate from the pampas,"
    On the shoot.

Those who love me call me little dynamite,
    I'm a pet,
I'm a walking, stalking terror of the night
    You can bet,
By my nickel plated teasers
Many a rusty featured Greaser's
    Sun has set.

Sometimes I strikes an unprotected town,
    Paint it red,
Choke the sheriff, turn the marshall upside down
    On his head,
Call for drinks for all the party
And if chinned by any smarty
    Pay in lead.

I'm a coyote of the sunset, "Pirate Dude!"
    Hear me zip;
In the company of gentlemen I'm rude
    With my lip,
Down in front remove that nigger
Or I'll perforate his figger,
    I am fly, I am fighter, I am flip.

32. *An Afternoon Like This*

(*Hoofs and Horns,* Tucson, Arizona. Vol. V, July 1935. P. 12.)

An afternoon like this it was in tough old Cherokee
An outlaw come a-hornin' in and asked who I might be.

He spun around his finger joint a six-gun primed with lead,
He yelled, "By Judas, answer quick!" And this is what I said:

"My Uncle Jess was Jesse James, my ma was Chalk Taw Sade,
Black Jack Ketchum was my pa, Sam Bass my cradle maid.

"They fed me fust on she wolf's milk and while my teeth
           was cuttin'
My rattle was a diamondback with twenty-seven buttons.

"I learned to bark before I talked, before I talked to swear,
I always used tarantulas to comb my shinin' hair.

"Where e'er I make my bed at night, the grass it fades and dies
And when I'm ridin' in the rain the fearful lightnin' shies."

33. *Bitter Creek*

(FAC II 327: manuscript, Colorado.)

I was born way over yonder
On the shores of Bitter Creek,
Where a self-respecting cactus wouldn't dwell,
And the sweet and gentle zephyrs
That fan your cheeks at night
Make hot boxes on the very hubs of hell.

I'm a killer from the desert
Strewn with dead things all around,
And the poison from my teeth is just a-purlin'.
I'm a hooded hydrophobia skunk;
My tail drags on the ground,
And I'm lookin' for some cuss to try and curl it.

I was suckled by a grizzly
And weaned on nigger gin.
Gila monsters was my playmates as a lad.
My guns turn blue by moonlight,
And the sparks fly off my teeth;
And in hot midsummer dog-days I go mad.

Line up, gents, and name your liquor,
Plant your hind feet on the rail;
Pour a quart of poison underneath your shirt,
'Fore my temper gets to smartin'
And my six-gun starts to barkin',
And I smoke your gol-durn village off the earth.

34. *Boomer Johnson*

The camp cook, on roundup or on trail herd, was probably the most influential man in the outfit after the foreman himself. This account of Boomer Johnson illustrates the point. (Henry Herbert Knibbs, *Songs of the Lost Frontier.* Boston and New York: Houghton Mifflin Co., 1930. Pp. 61–63. Copyright 1958 by Ida Julia Knibbs. Reprinted by permission of the publisher, Houghton Mifflin Company.)

Now Mr. Boomer Johnson was a gettin' old in spots,
But you don't expect a bad-man to go wrestlin' pans and pots;
But he'd done his share of killin' and his draw was gettin' slow,
So he quits a-punchin' cattle and he takes to punchin' dough.

Our foreman up and hires him, figurin' age had rode him tame,
But a snake don't get no sweeter just by changin' of its name.
Well, Old Boomer knowed his business — he could cook to make
    you smile,
But say, he wrangled fodder in a most peculiar style.

He never used no matches — left 'em layin' on the shelf;
Just some kerosene and cussin' and the kindlin' lit itself.
And, pardner, I'm allowin' it would give a man a jolt,
To see him stir *frijoles* with the barrel of his Colt.

Now killin' folks and cookin' ain't so awful far apart;
That must 'a' been why Boomer kept a-practicin' his art;
With the front sight of his pistol he would cut a pie-lid slick,
And he'd crimp her with the muzzle for to make the edges stick.

He built his doughnuts solid, and it sure would curl your hair,
To see him plug a doughnut as he tossed it in the air.
He bored the holes plumb center every time his pistol spoke,
Till the can was full of doughnuts and the shack was full of smoke.

We-all was gettin' jumpy — but he couldn't understand
Why his shootin' made us nervous when his cookin' was so grand.
He kept right on performin', and it weren't no big surprise,
When he took to markin' tombstones on the covers of his pies.

84

They didn't taste no better and they didn't taste no worse,
But a-settin' at that table was like ridin' in a hearse;
You didn't do no talkin' and you took just what you got,
So we et till we was foundered just to keep from gettin' shot.

Us at breakfast one bright mornin', I was feelin' kind of low,
When Old Boomer passed the doughnuts and I tells him plenty, "No!
All I takes this trip is coffee, for my stomach is a wreck,"
I could see the itch for killin' swell the wattles on his neck.

Scorn his grub? He strings some doughnuts on the muzzle of
        his gun,
And he shoves her in my gizzard and he says, "You're takin' one!"
He was set to start a graveyard, but for once he was mistook;
Me not wantin' any doughnuts, I just up and salts the cook.

Did they fire him? Listen, pardner, there was nothin' left to fire.
Just a row of smilin' faces and another cook to hire.
If he joined some other outfit and is cookin'—what I mean,
It's where they ain't no matches and they don't need kerosene.

35. *Étude Géographique*

With all the serious poetic efforts to elevate the cowboy into an idealized image of the westerner, it would be a pity if there were not, here and there, a tongue-in-cheek effort to debunk the myth. (Stoddard King, *What the Queen Said.* New York: George H. Doran Co., 1926. P. 62.)

Out West, they say, a man's a man; the legend still persists
That he is handy with a gun and careless with his fists.
The fact is, though, you may not hear a stronger word than "Gosh!"
From Saskatoon, Saskatchewan, to Walla Walla, Wash.

In western towns 'tis many years since it was last the rage
For men to earn their daily bread by holding up the stage,
Yet story writers still ascribe such wild and woolly bosh
To Saskatoon, Saskatchewan, and Walla Walla, Wash.

The gents who roam the West today are manicured and meek,
They shave their features daily and they bathe three times
      a week.
They tote the tame umbrella and they wear the mild galosh
From Saskatoon, Saskatchewan, to Walla Walla, Wash.

But though the West has frowned upon its old nefarious games,
It still embellishes the map with sweet, melodious names,
Which grow in lush profusion like the apple and the squash
From Saskatoon, Saskatchewan, to Walla Walla, Wash.

36. *The White Steed of the Prairies*

"Out of these conditions and facts grew the legend of the White Steed of the Prairies, that superb horse, a super-horse that had all the desirable and unusual qualities, all the speed, all the endurance, all the beauty that imagination could give him. Since he had all these attributes, everybody wanted him, but nobody could take him. He was ubiquitous, ethereal, a mere ideal, a phantom of the plainsman's mind, and he ranged from Canada to Mexico." — W. P. Webb. (W. P. Webb, "The White Steed of the Prairies." *Legends of Texas,* Publications of Texas Folklore Society, No. III [1924], pp. 223–26. Quoted from *The Democratic Review,* April 1843. Reprinted by permission of the Texas Folklore Society.) The author is J. Barber.

Mount, mount for the chase! let your lassos be strong,
And forget not sharp spur and tough buffalo thong;
For the quarry ye seek hath oft baffled, I ween,
Steeds swift as your own, backed by hunters as keen.

Fleet barb of the prairie, in vain they prepare
For thy neck, arched in beauty, the treacherous snare;
Thou wilt toss thy proud head, and with nostrils stretched wide,
Defy them again, as thou still hast defied.

Trained nags of the course, urged by rowel and rein,
Have cracked their strong thews in thy pursuit in vain;
While a bow-shot in front, without straining a limb,
The wild courser careered as 'twere pastime to him.

Ye may know him at once, though a herd be in sight,
As he moves o'er the plain like a creature of light —
His mane streaming forth from his beautiful form
Like the drift from a wave that has burst in the storm.

Not the team of the Sun, as in fable portrayed,
Through the firmament rushing in glory arrayed,
Could match, in wild majesty, beauty and speed,
That tireless, magnificent, snowy-white steed.

Continued

Much gold for his guerdon, promotion and fame,
Wait the hunter who captures that fleet-footed game;
Let them bid for his freedom, unbridled, unshod,
He will roam till he dies through these pastures of God.

And ye think on his head your base halters to fling!
So ye shall — when yon Eagle has lent you his wing;
But no slave of the lash that your stables contain
Can e'er force to a gallop the steed of the Plain!

His fields have no fence save the mountain and sky;
His drink the snow-capped *Cordilleras* supply;
'Mid the grandeur of nature sole monarch is he,
And his gallant heart swells with the pride of the free.

37. *The Broncho Buster*

The stubborn will of some horses, coupled with sheer muscular toughness, are qualities which have provoked and intrigued man more than any other animal has done. (Gordon 2531: manuscript.)

I've busted bronchos off and on ever since I struck the trail,
I have saddled bronchos from nostril down to tail,
But I struck one down on Powder River, and, Stranger,
    I'll be cussed,
'Twas the only living broncho that your servant couldn't bust.

He was a little no 'count buckskin and not worth two cents
    to keep,
With rims of white all 'round his eyes, and as woolly as
    a sheep:
With a black stripe down his back-bone and his heels he
    couldn't trust,
So I cinched the hull, an' I says, "Now, bronk, here's where
    you sure get bust."

I thought I'd struck a picnic, but, Stranger, I'll be cussed!
'Twas the bronk that had the picnic for he sort o' wouldn't bust,
When I got on he went so high that the lights from Zion shone.
Right there we parted company an' he come down alone.

When I at last struck turf again the broncho he was free;
I brought along a bunch of stars to dance in front of me.
The boss drug me to the river an' says, "Billy, now don't
    you croak,
For there's a five-spot comin' when this here bronk is broke."

I have no rich relations awaitin' me back East,
I am not ridin' air-ships or an electric flyin' beast,
I've sold my chaps and saddle, my spurs can lay and rust,
For once in a while there is a bronk that the Devil himself
    can't bust.

38. *Idaho Jack*

This poem may survive, not as great poetry, but for the manner in which it captures the drama and pageantry of the prime event in rodeos: bronc riding. It is said to have been written by "Powder River" Jack Lee. (Jack H. Lee, *West of the Powder River.* New York: Huntington Press, 1933. Pp. 59–60.)

Idaho Jack from the Salmon buttes
Grinned up at the buckaroos, workin' the chutes;
Feels of the cinch as he jerks up the slack
On the outlaw and mankiller, Red River Black:
Twists on the hackamore, tightens the noose
Yells to the punchers, "All set, turn 'im loose."
Down goes the lever and, bang, goes the bell,
And out comes a cowboy a-ridin' for hell.

The crowd's up and screamin' with deafenin' cheers,
For they're sightin' a ride they'll remember for years.
Snake River Dugan leaps up and he bawls,
"Watch that bowlegged rider from Idaho Falls."
The outlaw's a killer who knows no defeat,
But the rider's still with him and holdin' his seat;
His spurs rake the stallion, who's sunfishin' back.
But he don't know the rider called Idaho Jack.

There's hazers and clowns with their trick ridin' mules;
Team ropers, pick-ups, and bull-doggin' fools;
Chuckeaters, ranch hands, and tenderfeet proud,
Of the kind you will meet in a rodeo crowd.
Pens full of cattle from the desert and range,
A-frightened and bawlin' at scenes new and strange;
Waddies and gamblers on dust covered track
And the bets fifty-fifty on Idaho Jack.

There's yippin' and yellin' that reaches the skies,
But the cowboy don't hear for there's blood in his eyes.
On the mad fighting cayuse of sinew and bone
The rider from Idaho's holdin' his own.
When a roar and a shout bursts forth from the mob,
That starts with a cheer, and ends with a sob;
For the cinch breaks loose on Red River Black,
And down with the saddle comes Idaho Jack.

Like a flash, he's out from the hoofs below
As the stallion strikes with a killing blow,
Grazin' the saddle from horn to cinch,
And he gains his life by a half an inch.
The pick-ups are ready, and save his hide;
He rolls the "makin's" with mouth set wide;
Grins to the crowd, as he waddles back,
And shakes his fist at Red River Black.

39. *The Legend of Boastful Bill*

Boastful Bill's encounter with "the hawse from Idaho" poses a problem similar to the collision of the irresistible force with the immovable object. The indomitable will of a hero meets an impossible task head-on: for Bill the result is not defeat but unending struggle. (Charles Badger Clark, *Sun and Saddle Leather.* Boston: Richard G. Badger, 1920. Pp. 52–56. First edition 1915.)

At a roundup on the Gily,
  One sweet mornin' long ago,
Ten of us was throwed right freely
  By a hawse from Idaho.
And we thought he'd go a-beggin'
  For a man to break his pride
'Til, a-hitchin' up one leggin',
  Boastful Bill cut loose and cried—

    "I'm a on'ry proposition for to hurt;
    I fulfill my earthly mission with a quirt;
    I kin ride the highest liver
    'Tween the Gulf and Powder River,
    And I'll break this thing as easy as I'd flirt."

So Bill climbed the Northern Fury
  And they mangled up the air
Till a native of Missouri
  Would have owned his brag was fair.
Though the plunges kep' him reelin'
  And the wind it flapped his shirt,
Loud above the hawse's squealin'
  We could hear our friend assert:

    "I'm the one to take such rakin's as a joke.
    Some one hand me up the makin's of a smoke!
    If you think my fame needs bright'nin'
    W'y I'll rope a streak of lightnin'
    And I'll cinch 'im up and spur 'im till he's broke."

Then one caper of repulsion
  Broke that hawse's back in two.
Cinches snapped in the convulsion;
  Skyward man and saddle flew.
Up he mounted, never laggin',
  While we watched him through our tears,
And his last thin bit of braggin'
  Came a-droppin' to our ears:

    "If you'd ever watched my habits very close
    You would know I've broke such rabbits by the gross.
    I have kep' my talent hidin';
    I'm too good for earthly ridin'
    And I'm off to bust the lightnin',—
    Adios!"

Years have gone since that ascension.
  Boastful Bill ain't never lit,
So we reckon that he's wrenchin'
  Some celestial outlaw's bit.
When the night rain beats our slickers
  And the wind is swift and stout
And the lightnin' flares and flickers,
  We kin sometimes hear him shout:

    "I'm a bronco-twistin' wonder on the fly;
    I'm the ridin' son-of-thunder of the sky.
    Hi! you earthlin's, shut your winders
    While we're rippin' clouds to flinders.
    If this blue-eyed darlin' kicks at you, you die!"

Stardust on his chaps and saddle,
  Scornful still of jar and jolt,
He'll come back some day, astraddle
  Of a bald-faced thunderbolt.
And the thin-skinned generation
  Of that dim and distant day
Sure will stare with admiration
  When they hear old Boastful say—

    "I was first, as old rawhiders all confessed.
    Now I'm last of all rough riders, and the best.
    Huh, you soft and dainty floaters,
    With your a'roplanes and motors—
    Huh! Are you the great grandchildren of the West!"

40. *The Flying Outlaw*

Language and images of this poem fit the circumstances of range riding
in the Great Basin like a glove. Yet the poem rises above a mere epi-
sode of a puncher throwing his lasso at a prize wild stallion: the whole
existential dilemma of man is evoked — his futile élan towards cosmic
truth and discombobulation back into humdrum existence. The author
is Curley W. Fletcher. (*Songs of the Sage.* Los Angeles: Frontier Pub-
lishing Co., 1931. Pp. 60–64.)

Come gather 'round me, cowboys,
And listen to me clost
Whilst I tells yuh 'bout a mustang
That must uh been a ghost.

Yuh mighta heard of a cayuse
Uh the days they called 'em a steed
Thet spent his time with the eagles
And only come down fer his feed.

He goes by the name of Pegasus,
He has himself wings to fly;
He eats and drinks in the Bad Lands,
And ranges around in the sky.

Seems he belongs to an outfit,
Some sisters, The Muses, they say,
And they always kep 'im in hobbles
Till he busts 'em and gets away.

Fer years they tries hard to ketch 'im,
But he keeps right on runnin' free;
The riders wore way too much clothes then,
Cowboys was knights then, yuh see.

He sure bears a bad reputation,
I don't sabe how it begin,
Part eagle, part horse, and a devil;
They claims that he's meaner than sin.

I'm a-ridin that rimrock country
Up there around Wild Horse Springs,
And I like to fell out uh my saddle
When that bronk sails in on his wings.

I feels like I must be plumb crazy,
As I gazes up over a bank,
A-watchin' that albino mustang
Uh preenin' his wings as he drank.

Finally he fills up with water,
Wings folded, he starts in to graze,
And I notice he's headin' up my way
Where I straddle my horse in a daze.

And then I comes to, all excited,
My hands is a-tremblin' in hope,
As I reaches down on my saddle
And fumbles a noose in my rope.

Ready, I rides right out at him
Spurrin' and swingin' my loop
Before he can turn and get goin'
I throws — and it fits like a hoop.

I jerks out the slack and I dallies,
I turn and my horse throws him neat,
And he lets out a blood curdlin' beller
While I'm at him hogtyin' his feet.

I puts my hackamore on him,
And a pair uh blinds on his eyes;
I hobbles his wings tight together
So he can't go back to the skies.

I lets him up when he's saddled,
My cinch is sunk deep in his hide;
I takes the slack out uh my spur straps
'Cause it looks like a pretty tough ride.

Continued

I crawls him just like he was gentle,
I'm a little bit nervous you bet;
I feels pretty sure I can ride 'im,
I still has his wings hobbled yet.

I raises the blinds and he's snortin',
Then moves like he's walkin' on eggs;
He grunts and explodes like a pistol;
I see he's at home on his legs.

Wolves, and panthers, and grizzlies,
Centipedes, triantlers, and such;
Scorpins, snakes, and bad whiskey
Compared to him wasn't much.

I got a deep seat in my saddle
And my spurs both bogged in the cinch;
I don't aim to take any chances,
I won't let him budge me an inch.

He acts like he's plumb full uh loco,
Just ain't got a lick uh sense;
He's weavin' and buckin' so crooked
That I thinks of an Arkansaw fence.

I'm ridin' my best and I'm busy
And troubled a-keepin' my seat;
He didn't need wings fer flyin',
He's handy enough on his feet.

He's got me half blind and I weaken
He's buckin' around in big rings;
Besides which he kep' me a-guessin',
A-duckin', and dodgin' his wings.

By golly he starts gettin' rougher,
He's spinnin' and sunfishin', too,
I grabs me both hands full uh leather;
I'm weary and wishin' he's through.

He hits on the ground with a twister
That broke the wing hobbles, right there;
Before I can let loose and quit him,
We're sailin' away in the air.

He smoothes out and keeps on a climbin'
Till away down, miles below,
I gets me a look at the mountains
And the peaks all covered with snow.

Up through the clouds, I'm a-freezin',
Plumb scared and I'm dizzy to boot;
I sure was a-wishin' I had me
That thing called a paramachute.

And then I musta gone loco,
Or maybe I goes sound asleep,
'Cause when I wakes up I'm a-layin'
Right down on the ground in a heap.

He may uh had wings like an angel
And he may uh been light on his feet,
But he oughta had horns like the devil
And a mouth fit fer eatin' raw meat.

I've lost a good saddle and bridle,
My rope and some other good things,
But I'm sure glad to be here to tell yuh
To stay off uh horses with wings.

41. *Epitaphs for Horses*

. . . in little corners of the West, under spreading yellow pines, or amid the piñons, or at the points of aspen groves, not with extreme infrequency, appeared boards, or else slabs of slate, either of them rudely inscribed by heated iron or by scratching metal point. Their legends varied with the stories they had to tell, often were illiterately phrased, but occasionally disclosed assistance by some scholar among the regretful cowboy's friends. Three of them read respectively as follows:

JIM
a reel hors
Oct 1, 82

HERE LIES
"I'M HERE"
The Very Best of Cow Ponies,
A Gallant, Little Gentleman.
Died on this Spot, Sept. 3, 1890

HERE LIES
"WHAT NEXT"
Born ——, ——, 1886, at ——.
Died July 16, 1892, near Ft. Washakie, Wyo.
He had the Body of a Horse,
The Spirit of a Knight, and
The Devotion of the Man
Who Erected this Stone."

42. *The Mule*

A bit of lyricism coupled with frustration suffered at the hooves of a recalcitrant mule. (JL 204: manuscript.)

Oh, the cow puncher loves the whistle of his rope
   As he races over the plains,
And the stage driver loves the popping of his whip
   And the jingle of his Concord chains.

And we'll all pray the Lord that we will be saved
   And will keep the Golden Rule,
But I'd rather be home with the girl I love
   Than to monkey with this God-damned mule.

43. *The Stampede*

In this treatment of a cattle stampede, one of the cowboy's most dangerous and dramatic experiences, interest is focused upon the stamina and sure-footedness of the cow ponies: men and mounts all prove their worth though the gray-haired man on an indomitable roan wins first laurels. The author is Arthur L. Caldwell. (O. W. Coursey, *Literature of South Dakota*. Mitchell, S. D.: Educator Supply Co., 4th ed., 1925. Pp. 207–8.)

The red sun breaks through muddy lakes of haze and rifted cloud,
And still and gray the prairies lay as motionless as the shroud.
But a distant roar was on the air, a rumble from afar,
And a dust cloud brown was sweeping down from the blue
      horizon's bar.

Above the line the great horns shine, beneath, the sharp
      hoofs speed,
And the solid ground shakes with the sound of a herd in
      full stampede.
And close to the lead is a coal-black steed, and a boy with a
      dashing bay,
Then a man with a roan who rides alone, whose hair is streaked
      with gray.

While the West still glowed they mounted and rode, and the
      reckless race began,
Through the dim starlight of the prairie night, and still they
      galloped on,
For life is cheap when men must keep these runaway brutes beside,
And until they stop, or the horses drop, it is ride and ride and ride.

The sun, from high in a murky sky, shines hot on the dusty track
Where two men ride by the great herd's side, still led by the
      fiery black;
An hour ago on the treacherous slough the gallant bay went down,
And a young voice clear rang out a cheer for the men who
      galloped on.

And now the black is falling back, panting, with low-hung head,
And shortening strides, though his dust-gray sides the spurs have
      marked with red.
He is out of the race, but into his place the gray-haired rider sweeps,
And foot by foot and inch by inch to the head of the herd he creeps.

And along the flank of the surging rank, over the trampling noise,
The echoes break as his pistols speak in sharp and threatening voice,
Till the danger is past, and they turn at last, with heavy,
      plunging tread,
Tired and blown, and the plucky roan swings slowly 'round ahead.

Give praise to the old gray veteran bold, who turned the
      maddened throng
Nor let it lack for the man with the black, who held the lead
      so long;
But what shall we add of the bare-faced lad, who knew that his race
      was done,
When, helpless, he lay by his fallen bay, but cheered his
      comrades on?

44. *The Wrangler Kid*

Grass fires, out of hand, were a threat to both man and beast. Here cowboys are trapped by encircling flames: a deep gully—escape to the men but not to their hobbled horses. The Wrangler Kid's heroic deed consists in his risk of death and actual disfigurement to cut the horses loose. (Hendren 278: manuscript.)

The grass fire swooped like a red wolf pack,
    On the wings of a west wind dry.
It's red race left the scorched plains black
    'Neath a sullen, smoky sky.

And the wagon boss of the Bar-Y-Cross
    He rallied his roisterous crew.
"Boys, shoot some steers, and hang the loss,
    An' split them smack in two!"

They split six steers, with the blood side down,
    They dragged them to and fro.
But the grass fire laughed like a demon clown
    At a devil's three-ringed show.

The flame draft drove like a wind from hell,
    Across the drags they drew.
"It's no use boys!" came the foreman's yell.
    "She's roarin' right on through."

They scattered, then, from the headfires path,
    To close in from the sides,
And some stayed on to fight its wrath,
    Some fled to save their hides.

Now one who stayed was the Wrangler Kid,
    His whisker fuzz scorched black,
And he battled hard, as the others did,
    But the fire still pushed them back.

It pushed them back as the wind veered round,
    Till trapped, they faced its sweep,
At the edge of a gully that split the ground,
    Too wide for a horse to leap.

'Twas down from the saddle dropped boss and men,
    And into the gulley they fled.
Safe now the men, but their horses then
    Were left to the grass fire's hell.

What! lives there a man who loves life less
    Than the dumb-brute horse he rides?
The Wrangler Kid stayed shelterless
    On the bank at the horses' side.

And he cut them free from the drags they drew,
    Through the flames he spurred alone.
To-day the Kid bears scars, 'tis true,
    Brands of the Red God's own.

45. *Going West*

Undisguised maudlin lyricism is at a low order of value among literary critics of our day: not so among the folk who purge their souls concerning their most poignant experiences by the singing of songs such as this. (FAC I 460: No. 69A, Archive of Folk Song, Library of Congress.)

I'm going out West before long,
I'm going out West before long,
I'm going out West where times are best,
I'm going out West before long.

My boy, he's gone West, turn back, turn back,
My boy, he's gone West, turn back, turn back,
My boy, he's gone West and he'll never come back,
I'm going out West before long.

Don't cry, little girl, don't cry,
Don't cry, little girlie, don't cry,
Little girlie, don't cry when I tell you good-by,
Oh, I'm going out West before long.

Do you know what you promised me?
Do you know what you promised me?
You promised me you'd marry me,
I'm going out West before long.

Oh lay your hand in mine,
Oh lay your hand in mine,
Lay your hand in mine and say you'll be mine,
I'm a-going out West before long.

46. *The Good Old Days of Adam and Eve*

Doggerel on the universal theme of the decadence of the younger generation: for those who actually pioneered in the West there is some justification, since life was indeed easier for their children and grandchildren than it had been for them. (PC-F 78: manuscript.)

When I was young and went to a ball
We had an ox-sled or no team at all,
And now we must have a horse and sleigh,
Buffalo robes and everything gay.

> *Sing heigh, sing lo, I can but grieve*
> *For the good old days of Adam and Eve.*

The girls they didn't puff and flought
If they had one dress they were all ragged-out.
And now they haul their dresses so tight across the back
They look like a punkin tied up in a sack.

> *Sing . . .*

The boys they used to be hardy and gay
And to work both night and day,
But now they look like an eel that's skinned,
Rattle like a corn-stalk shaking in the wind.

> *Sing . . .*

When I was young and very little
We used to have a meeting house 'thout any steeple,
But now they must have a steeple and a bell
And if you don't go to meeting you will surely go to — well!

> *Sing . . .*

47. *The Campfire Has Gone Out*

Every generation of "senior citizens" has bemoaned the passing of the forms, institutions, and values that gave meaning to their own years of vigor and action. This poem, by Ben Arnold, fits the circumstances like an old shoe, and has the same kind of folksy beaten-up charm. (Lewis F. Crawford, *Rekindling Campfires*. Bismark, N. D.: Capitol Book Co., 1926. Pp. 309–10.)

Through progress of the railroads our occupation's gone;
We'll get our ideas into words, our words into a song.
First comes the cowboy—he's the spirit of the West;
Of all the pioneers I claim the cowboys are the best;
We'll miss him in the round-up, it's gone, his merry shout,
The cowboy has left the country, his campfire has gone out.

You freighters, our companions, you've got to leave this land;
Can't drag your loads for nothing through the gumbo, and the sand;
The railroads are bound to beat you—so do your level best,
Give it up to the granger and strike out farther west.
Bid them all adieu and give the merry shout,—
"The cowboy has left the country and his campfire has gone out."

When I think of those good old days my eyes with tears will fill;
When I think of the tin can by the fire and the coyote on the hill,
I'll tell you, boys, in those days old-timers stood a show,—
Our pockets full of money, not a sorrow did we know;
But, how times have changed since then, we're poorly clothed
        and fed;
Our wagons are all broken down and horses most all dead.

Soon we'll leave this country, then you'll hear the angels shout,
"Oh, here they come to Heaven, their campfire has gone out."

48. *Shootin' Up the Trail*

This has the same general tone as the preceding poem except that there is an illumination of greater historic depth: awareness that even beyond the period "when the land was young" for Anglo-Americans an accumulation of human and animal activity had deposited its silt of myth upon the landscape. The author is Grant L. Shumway. (FAC III 127: newspaper clipping.)

They are shootin' the rocks in the Mitchell Gap
　Where once we rode when the land was young.
We almost wish that the new-fangled yap
　Who figured improvin' that road—was hung.

This shootin' of holes in the Oregon Trail
　Where a million traveled across the land;
This rippin' the California Trail
　Where more of them went to the golden sand;

Makes us plumb sick—Old Pinto and me.
　Say—old "paint" hoss—lend me your ear:
Do you like the looks of the thing you see?
　Do you like their smoke? Or the engineer?

In the old trail days the endless stream
　Moved on and on to the setting sun,
And each had his own particular dream
　Of what was what when the trailin' was done.

And the women who pushed their baby carts
　Two thousand miles to the mountain nest,
Left in this valley a "Trail of Hearts"
　And consecrated to love and rest.

The Pass was found by the buffalo;
　The Indian followed across its rim;
The trapper traveled it to and fro
　So long ago that the years are dim.

We did not know why the red men clung
　To the mountain side with a lingering hope;
Why the red brave fought; and the red man sung
　While weaving flowers along its slope.

Continued

But we sure know now—when we hear a roar
 And rocks are torn from where they may be.
The powder a-rippin' the mountain core
 Is tearin' the heart of Pinto and me.

The Pony Express and Overland streams
 Went flying along ere the days of gas,
And ten-ton wagons and ten-mule teams
 Went over the trail through Mitchell Pass.

We rode the Trail in the round-up days
 When Coad first started to build a fence.
We dragged his pole-bars every ways
 Because we hated to see it commence.

But the March of Time and the ruthless folk
 Who never have known of the open range
Have fenced us in—but spirit unbroke,
 We'll watch the swift procession of change.

Now we have a boulevard through the Pass
 For softie buddies with motor cars;
With cushion springs and shades and glass
 And the maniac speed of shooting stars.

So, Pinto! the cockeys of new-born days,
 The commerce guys and the speedier class
And the wrecking crew have had their ways
 By shootin' the rocks in the Mitchell Pass.

49. *The Old Ute Trail*

The writer here gets to the roots of the western myth: bison, deer, Indians, and trappers, whose ghosts form a silent and unseen audience for the passage of the cold metalic creations of our insensitive generation. (Hendren 400: manuscript.)

Ghosts of the Utes look down on this trail
    Which white man's magic has made smooth and wide,
They watch with awe as chariots of steel
    Go winding swiftly up the mountain side.

The picture fades. They see again the trail
    The red man used before the white man came—
Worn by the moccasins of centuries,
    Marked by the countless feet of roving game.

Here passed the deer, and here passed the buffalo.
    Climbed when the sun god drove them from the plain
Toward high green valleys and cool mountain streams,
    Here in the fall the game passed down again.

Here climbed the Utes; the women with their packs.
    The chieftains on their ponies riding slow
Up the steep canyon following their game
    Toward pastures watered by eternal snow.

Here passed the mountain trappers in their day,
    Here wagons rumbled in the rush for gold,
To Tarryall, Fairplay and Buckskin Joe—
    By day or night, the trail was never cold.

And now the way is shaped to modern needs,
    Widened, the road becomes a smooth highway;
The buffalo have gone, but painted ghosts
    Still guard the game trail of the bygone day.

50. *Ballade of Boot-Hill*

This is a lament for the passing of the badman, and somewhat more: the badman becomes symbolic of men of violent freedom displaced by a generation of slaves to cold, metallic, antibiotic creations. (*Hobo News,* Fol. 7, by W. A. Ward.)

In the silent tombs the killers sleep,
   On naked sun burnt desert land,
While over head the sand storms sweep,
   And cactus guard the shifting sand.
They were a daring dauntless band
   With nerve to meet the small or great,
The men who bet a fifty grand
   When Texas was a two-gun state.

   Sleep, killers, in Boot Hill's sod,
   The men who knew the song of hate
   And fought and died with shooting rod,
   When Texas was a two-gun state.

Gone are the bad men of the West,
   And gone are monte, stud, and draw;
The faro man has dealt his best,
   And gone with him is six-gun law.
Yes, gone are the days when life was raw,
   And men would jump at ruthless fate,
Though Death stood watch with grinning maw,
   When Texas was a two-gun state.

The gunmen sleep in Boot Hill grim,
   While over head fast aeroplanes sail
And on the road, a paving gem
   That was once but a cattle trail,
A horseless cart that needs no rail
   Is speeding at breathless rate,
But Boot Hill knew a somber tale,
   When Texas was a two-gun state.

51. *Further West*

Here the "mythogenesis" of the West has come full-circle: it emerges as the site of man's wildest and hence unfulfilled and unfulfillable dreams. (Hendren 683: newspaper clipping.)

There's a country famed in story as you've often times been told,
'Tis a land of mighty rivers flowing over sands of gold;
The abode of peace and plenty, and with quietness 'tis blest,
But this country that's so famous is away off in the West.

Once a man in Androscogin or in some outlandish place
With a view to find that country to the westward set his face.
He was weary at Chicago, so he sat him down to rest,
But 'twas only there the centre, not the fabled golden West.

So he crossed the rolling prairies, stretching onward like the sea;
"I am bound to find that country if there's such a one," said he.
So he swam the Mississippi, soon upon Missouri's breast
He explored the wilds of Kansas for this country in the West.

Climbing o'er the Rocky Mountains, on he kept his weary way,
'Til the broad Pacific waters right before his vision lay.
Then he sat him down and pondered but for him there was no rest,
"Surely 'tis an island," said he, "that fair country in the West."

So a vessel quick he builded and the shore he left behind,
Sailing on with eager longing still his happy isle to find.
After many days one morning he beheld the wished-for land,
Steering 'mid the shoals and breakers quick he reached the
          golden strand.

From his gallant bark he landed, wading through the seething foam
With his eyes wide ope' with wonder for he found himself at home.
Thus he learned that one forever might go on and never rest
Still he would not find that country—for 'tis always further West.

52. *The Texas Ranger*

It is ironical that one of the best illustrations of the cult of "momism" in the literature of the American West is offered by the best known song of the Texas Rangers, whose unmitigated militancy against Indians and Mexicans is so well known. Perhaps the isolation and violence of a military campaign have a way of turning men's thoughts toward the security and biological warmth of infancy. There are scores of parodies of this song, each with its own particular treatment of the cult of perfect womanhood. (FAC II 462: from Herbert Halpert, New York Folksong Collection, 1938. Used with permission of Herbert Halpert.)

Come all you Texas rangers, pray listen unto me
While I'll relate the hardships as you may plainly see.
My name is nothing extra; the truth to you I'll tell,
I am a Texas ranger; brave boys, I wish you well.

'Twas at the age of brave sixteen I joined this jovial band
We marched from Saratoga down to the Rio Grande.
Our captain, he gave orders, I'm sure he thought it right,
"Before we reach the station, boys, you've got to fight."

I saw those Indians coming with their daggers in their hands,
My feelings at that moment no tongue could understand.
I saw their glittering glances as their arrows round me sailed,
My heart sank within me, my courage almost failed.

I saw the smoke a-rising, ascending to the skies,
My feelings at that moment, thought now was my time to die.
Our captain, he gave orders, I'm sure he gave command,
"To arms! To arms!" he shouted, "and by your horses stand."

For five hours we fought the battle until the fight was o'er,
Of all the dead and wounded I never had seen before.
Five hundred bold Texas rangers as ever trod the West
Lay bleeding there next morning with a death wound on their
      breast.

I thought of my dear mother who in tears to me did say,
"To you they are but strangers, with me you'd better stay."
But I thought she were old and childish and that she didn't know,
My mind was bent on rambling and a-rambling I did go.

There was a handsome maiden; she drew close to my side,
There she promised bravely that she would be my bride.
I kissed away the falling tear from her dark and bluish eye,
Told her I'd prove faithful, my love could never die.

Perhaps you've got a mother, perhaps a sister too,
Perhaps you've got a sweetheart to weep and mourn for you.
If this be your condition I advise you never to roam:
I have learnt this by experience, you had better stay at home.

My daddy and my mammy is on this earth no more,
My daddy and my mammy is on the golden shore.
The reason why I ramble, of course you'll plainly see,
I have got no wife nor sweetheart to weep and mourn for me.

Come you that stand around me, pray listen unto me,
Don't leave your home, your happy home, for gold nor poverty,
To be bound from friends and home on the dark and dreary plains
Where the Indians will leave you to never return again.

I've seen the fruits of rambling and I know their hardships well,
I've been in many a foreign fold where many a brave boy fell,
For me I will go home to the girl that I loved so well.

53. *Custer's Last Fight*

Again in a military ballad we encounter the cult of ideal womanhood. The annihilation of Custer's whole force is dwarfed in its importance by the tragedy of a wife and a mother not receiving last messages of loved ones because neither soldier survives. (FAC II 50: Arkansas files, WPA Writers Project, Library of Congress, 1936.)

It was just before George Custer's last fight
    Two soldiers drew their reins,
With a clasping hand, a parting word,
    For they never might meet again.

One had blue eyes and curly hair,
    Nineteen but a month ago,
He had red on his cheeks and down on his chin,
    He was only a boy, you know.

The other was tall and dark and strong
    But his faith in this world was dim;
He only trusted in those whom he loved,
    They were all the world to him.

"I have a picture in my heart,
    I will wear it in the fight,
A picture that is all this world to me,
    And it shines like the morning light.

"Like a morning light was her love to me,
    And she cherished my lonely life.
It was little I cared for the frown on her face
    When she promised to be my wife.

"Write to her, Charlie, when I am gone;
    Send back this fond fair face,
Tell her gently how I died,
    And where is my resting place."

Tears filled the eyes of the blue-eyed boy,
  And his heart was filled with pain,
Saying, "I'll do your bidding, comrade mine,
  If we never meet again.

"But if I get killed and you return,
  You must do as much for me.
I have a mother dear at home —
  Write her tenderly.

"She has lost us all one by one,
  Husband and son after son,
And I was the last of all her boys
  To answer the country's call."

Just then the order came to charge,
  For an instant hand touched hand.
The last goodbye — then onward rode
  That brave devoted band.

They rode together to the crest of the hill,
  When the red skins shot like hail,
Poured death among the ranks of the little band,
  And scalped them as they fell.

They rode up the hill they could not gain,
  Against a dark and gathering gloom,
And the few that were left of the gallant band,
  Rode slowly back again.

And among the dead that were left behind
  Was the boy with the curly hair;
And the tall dark boy that rode by his side
  Lay dead beside him there.

So none was left to tell the girl
  The last words her lover had said,
And the patient mother that was left at home
  Will learn that her boy is dead.

54. *Witch of the Canyon*

When his ladylove is absent, the lonely cowboy is able to conjure up the image of a mounted beauty who mysteriously appears at a desert water stop, greets the passengers, and then vanishes into nothingness. (Hendren 221: manuscript.)

Naught do I know of her birth and name,
Whither she vanished or whence she came;
But ever her echoing laughter
From the desert trail to the canyon walls
Tauntingly, hauntingly calls me back
To a drab little town by a pond-wet track —
A few line shacks and signal tower
Where the Limited stops for only an hour.

Skimming the sage like wind-blown flame,
Pinto and red-haired rider came,
Cantered and capered along the rail,
Greeted the train crew's jubilant hail,
With a light flung Stetson flung in air,
With a toss of her sun drenched hair
And a vibrant call from her throat
As sweet as a wild bird's mating note.

The passengers cheered as the pony pranced,
Her gay voice and blue eyes danced.
One breathless moment she tarried,
Then she whirled and raced for the trail again.
She whirled a kiss, her fingers spread,
The streaking blaze of her golden head,
Elfin laughter and wild bird's call
Echoing from the canyon wall.

55. *Broncho versus Bicycle*

Practical jokes and verse about them are often encountered in cowboy and western literature: the dude, tenderfoot, or other outsider is typically the "fall guy." Not so in this pseudo-primitive poem in which a dude from "Bosting" riding a "wheel with a crooked tail" beats a puncher on his best mount in a ten-mile race. Phonetic dialectal orthography is one of the characteristics of pseudo-primitive style. The poem is solidly in the genre of mass media advertising. The author is Captain Jack Crawford. (*Lariattes: A Book of Poems and Favorite Recitations.* Sigourney, Iowa: William A. Bell, 1904. Pp. 72–76.)

The first we saw of the high-tone tramp
War over thar' at our Pecos camp;
He war comin' down the Santa Fe trail
Astride of a wheel with a crooked tail,
A-skinnin' along with a merry song,
An' ringin' a little warnin' gong.
He looked so outlandish, strange and queer
That all of us grinned from ear to ear,
An' every boy on the round-up swore
He had never seed sich a hoss afore.

Continued

Wal, up he rode, with a sunshine smile,
A-smokin' a cigarette, an' I'll
Be kicked in the neck if I ever seen
Sich a saddle as that on his queer machine.
Why, it made us laugh, for it wasn't half
Big enough for the back of a suckin' calf.
He tuk our fun in a keerless way,
A-venturin' only once to say
Thar wasn't a broncho about the place
Could down that wheel in a ten-mile race.

I'd a lightnin' broncho out in the herd
That could split the air like a flyin' bird,
An' I hinted round in an off-hand way
That, pervidin' the enterprise'd pay,
I thought as I might jest happen to light
On a hoss that'd leave 'im out o' sight.
In less'n a second we seed 'im yank
A roll o' greenbacks out of his flank,
An' he said, if we wanted to bet, to name
The limit, an' he would tackle the game.

Just a week afore we had all been down
On a jamboree to the nearest town,
An' the whiskey joints, an' the faro games,
An' shakin' our hoofs wi' the dance-house dames
Made a wholesale bust; an', pard, I'll be cussed
If a man in the outfit had any dust;
An' so I explained, but the youth replied
That he'd lay the money matter aside.

An' to show that his back didn't grow no moss
He'd bet his machine again' my hoss.
I tuk him up, and the bet war closed,
An' me a-chucklin', fur I supposed
I war playin' in dead sure winnin' luck,
In the softest snap I had ever struck;
An' the boys chipped in with a knowin' grin,
For they thought the fool had no chance to win.

An' so we agreed fur to run that day
To the Navajo Crossin' ten miles away—
As han'some a track as ever you seed
For testin' a hoss's purtiest speed,
Apache Johnson and Texas Ned
Saddled their horses and rode ahead
To station themselves ten miles away,
To act as judges and see fair play,
While Mexican Bart and Big Jim Hart
Stayed back for to give us an even start.

I got aboard of my broncho bird,
An' we came to the scratch an' got the word.
An' I laughed till my mouth spread from ear to ear
To see that tenderfoot drop to the rear.

The first three miles slipped away first-rate,
Then broncho began fur to lose his gait;
But I wa'n't oneasy, an' didn't mind,
With tenderfoot more'n a mile behind.
So I jogged along, with a cowboy song,
Till all of a suddnt I heard that gong
A-ringin' a warnin' in my ear,
Ting! Ting! Ting! Ting! too infernal near,
An' lookin' back'ards I seed the chump
Of a tenderfoot gainin' every jump.

I hit ol' broncho a cut wi' the quirt,
An' once more got him to scratchin' dirt,
But his wind seemed weak, an' I tell you, boss,
I seed that he wasn't no ten-mile hoss.
Still the plucky brute took another shoot
An' pulled away from the wheel galoot.
But the animal couldn't hold his gait,
An' somehow the idee entered my pate
That if tenderfoot's legs didn't lose their grip
He'd own that hoss at the end o' the trip.

Continued

Close and closer come tenderfoot,
An' harder the whip to the hoss I put;
But the Eastern cuss, with a smile on his face,
Ran up to my side with his easy pace—
Rode up to my side, an', durn his hide,
Remarked 'twar a pleasant day fur a ride;
Then axed, onconsarned, if I had a match,
An' on his breeches give it a scratch,
Lit a cigarette, said he wished me good day,
An', as fresh as a daisy, scooted away.

Ahead he went—that infernal gong
A-ringin' "Good-by" as he flew along;
An' the smoke of his cigarette came back
Like a vapory snicker along the track.
On an' on he sped, gettin' further ahead,
His feet keepin' up that onceasable tread,
Till he faded away in the distance; an' when
I seed the condemned Eastern rooster again,
He war thar with the boys at the end of the race,
That same keerless, unconsarned smile on his face.

Now, pard, w'en a cowboy gits beat he don't sw'ar,
Nor kick, if the beatin' are done on the squar';
So I tuk that Easterner right by the hand,
An' told him that broncho awaited his brand.
Then I asked 'im his name, and whar from he came,
And how long he'd practised the wheel-rollin' game.
Tom Stevens, he said, war his name, an' he come
From a town they call Bosting, in ol' Yankeedom;
Then he jist paralyzed us by sayin' he'd whirled
That very identical wheel round the world.
Wal, pard, thar's the story o' how that smart chap
Done me up, w'en I thought I had sich a soft snap;
Done me up on a race with remarkable ease,
An' lowered my pride a good many degrees.

Did I give 'im the hoss? W'y, of course I did, boss,
An' I'll tell you it wa'n't no diminutive loss.
He writ me a letter from back in the East,
An' said He'd presented the neat, little beast
To a feller named Pope, who stands at the head
O' the ranch whar the cussed wheel horses ar' bred.

I've had other letters a-sayin' as how
Them crooked-tail wheels isn't in it, fur now
They're makin' a new-fangled sort of affair
With big rubber tires stuffed with nothing but air—
"Noomatics" they say is their name, an' they lay
Them high-up giraffe machines out o' the way;
An' as fur their speed, so the Stevens man writ,
"A streak o' greased lightnin' ain't in it a bit."
Thar's nothin', I'm thinkin', kin foller them things
In the way of surprisin' inventions but wings.

56. *The Cowboy*

This poem will bear reading several times; it is tightly charged with the images and deeds that make the mythical image of the cowboy. It is remarkable that such an orchestration of myth should have been possible already in the 1880s when real life-and-blood cowboys had existed less than twenty years. The author is John Antrobus. (*Montana Live-Stock Journal,* May 5, 1888.)

"What care I, what cares he,
What cares the world of the life we know?
Little they reck of the shadowless plains,
The shelterless mesa, the sun and the rains,
The wild, free life, as the winds that blow."
　　With his broad *sombrero,*
　　His worn *chapparejos,*
　　　　And clinking spurs;
　　Like a Centaur he speeds,
　　Where the wild bull feeds;
And he laughs ha, ha! — who cares, who cares!

Ruddy and brown, careless and free —
A king in the saddle — he rides at will
O'er the measureless range where rarely change
The smart gray plains so weird and strange,
Treeless, and streamless, and wondrous still!
　　With his slouch *sombrero,*
　　His torn *chapparejos,*
　　　　And clinking spurs;
　　Like a Centaur he speeds,
　　Where the wild bull feeds:
And he laughs ha, ha! — who cares, who cares!

He of the towns, he of the East,
Has only a vague, dull thought of him;
In his far off dreams, the cowboy seems
A mythical thing, a thing he deems
A Hun or a Goth as swart and grim!
    With his stained *sombrero,*
    His rough *chapparejos,*
        And clinking spurs;
    Like a Centaur he speeds,
    Where the wild bull feeds;
And he laughs ha, ha!—who cares, who cares!

Often alone, his saddle a throne,
He scans like a sheik the numberless herd;
Where the buffalo grass and the sage brush dry
In the hot white glare of a cloudless sky;
And the music of streams is never heard.
    With his gay *sombrero,*
    His brown *chapparejos,*
        And clinking spurs;
    Like a Centaur he speeds,
    Where the wild bull feeds,
And he laughs ha, ha!—who cares, who cares!

Swift and strong, and ever alert,
Yet sometimes he rests on the dreary vast;
And his thoughts, like the thoughts of other men,
Go back to his childhood days again,
And many a loved one in the past,
    With his gay *sombrero,*
    His rude *chapparejos,*
        And clinking spurs;
    He rests awhile,
    With a tear and a smile,
And he laughs ha, ha!—who cares, who cares!

Continued

Sometimes his mood from solitude
Hurries him, heedless off to town!
Where mirth and wine through the goblet shine,
And treacherous sirens twist and twine
The lasso that often brings him down;
    With his soaked *sombrero,*
    His rent *chapparejos,*
        And clinking spurs;
    He staggers back
    On the homeward track,
And shouts to the plains — who cares, who cares!

On the broncho's back he sways and swings
Yet mad and wild with the city's tune;
His pace is the pace of the song he sings,
And the ribald oath that maudlin clings
Like the wicked stench of the harlot's room,
    With his ragged *sombrero,*
    His torn *chapparejos,*
        His rowel-less spurs;
    He dashes amain
    Through the trackless rain;
Reeling and reckless — who cares, who cares!

'Tis over late at the ranchman's gate —
He and his fellows, perhaps a score,
Halt in a quarrel o'er night begun,
With a ready blow and a random gun —
There's a dead, dead companion! nothing more,
    With his slouched *sombrero,*
    His dark *chapparejos,*
        And clinking spurs;
    He dashes past,
    With face o'ercast,
And growls in his throat — who cares, who cares!

Away on the range there is little change;
He blinks in the sun, he herds the steers;
But a trail on the wind keeps close behind,
And whispers that stagger and blanch the mind
Through the hum of the solemn noon he hears
    With his dark *sombrero,*
    His stained *chapparejos,*
       His clinking spurs;
    He slides down
    Where the grasses brown
May hide his face, while he sobs — who cares!

But what care I, and what cares he —
This is the strain, common at least;
He is free and vain of his bridle-rein,
Of his spurs, of his gun, of the dull gray plain;
He is ever vain of his broncho beast!
    With his gray *sombrero,*
    His brown *chapparejos,*
       And clinking spurs;
    Like a Centaur he speeds,
    Where the wild bull feeds;
And he laughs ha, ha! — who cares, who cares!

Part Three

Dramatic Situations

and Events

PART III

Dramatic Situations and Events

57. Jim Bludso of the Prairie Belle

The studied primitivism of this poem about a fire aboard a Mississippi steamer is typical of scores of cowboy and western ballads. Bludso's code—duty, craftsmanship, forthright Gallic amorality—is typical of men of the first and second generations in the West. The last line about "a man who dies for men" has the stature of epic poetry. (John Hay, *The Pike County Ballads*. Boston: Houghton Mifflin Co., 1871, 1890, 1912. Pp. 9–12.)

Wall, no! I can't tell whar he lives,
  Because he don't live, you see;
Leastways, he's got out of the habit
  Of livin' like you and me.
Whar have you been for the last three year
  That you haven't heard folks tell
How Jimmy Bludso passed in his checks
  The night of the Prairie Belle?

He weren't no saint,—them engineers
  Is all pretty much alike,—
One wife in Natchez-under-the-Hill
  And another one here, in Pike;
A keerless man in his talk was Jim,
  And an awkward hand in a row,
But he never flunked, and he never lied,—
  I reckon he never knowed how.

And this was all the religion he had,—
  To treat his engine well;
Never be passed on the river;
  To mind the pilot's bell;
And if ever the Prairie Belle took fire,—
  A thousand times he swore,
He'd hold her nozzle agin the bank
  Till the last soul got ashore.

All boats has their day on the Mississip,
  And her day come at last,—
The Movastar was a better boat,
  But the Belle she *wouldn't* be passed.

Continued

And so she come tearin' along that night—
  The oldest craft on the line—
With a nigger squat on her safety-valve,
  And her furnace crammed, rosin and pine.

The fire bust out as she clared the bar,
  And burnt a hole in the night,
And quick as a flash she turned, and made
  For that willer-bank on the right.
There was runnin' and cursin', but Jim yelled out,
  Over all the infernal roar,
"I'll hold her nozzle agin the bank
  Till the last galoot's ashore."

Through the hot, black breath of the burnin' boat
  Jim Bludso's voice was heard,
And they all had trust in his cussedness,
  And knowed he would keep his word.
And, sure's you're born, they all got off
  Afore the smokestacks fell,—
And Bludso's ghost went up alone
  In the smoke of the Prairie Belle.

He weren't no saint,—but at jedgment
  I'd run my chance with Jim,
'Longside of some pious gentlemen
  That wouldn't shook hands with him.
He seen his duty, a dead-sure thing,—
  And went for it thar and then;
And Christ ain't a going to be too hard
  On a man that died for men.

58. *Old North*

We place Old North alongside Paul Bunyan's Blue Ox as a mythical image of oxen that served man in the opening of the West. The author is N. Howard Thorp. (*Songs of the Cowboys*. Boston: Houghton Mifflin Co., 1921. Pp. 117–8.)

When the Mormons drifted southward he was one of a
    ten-span team,
The biggest young ox them Utah bullwhackers had ever seen.

Tawny an' bony an' holler, at three years full six feet tall,
An' he'd break the chain whenever he'd strain in a heavy
    wagon stall.

Out of a team of twenty which died in the White Sands Pass,
He alone pulled through an' made his way to the springs of
    San Nicolas.

Twenty Mormon women, in all, fifty Mormon souls,
Died from the lack of water, paying the desert toll.

The ranchmen on hearing the story, how everyone had died,
Let the big steer have his freedom through the Organ Valley wide.

In the winter he'd drift down southward to the Franklin
    Mountains warm;
In the summer you'd find him grazin' on the top of El Toro's horn.

59. Californy Stage

The adversities of western travel in years preceding the railroad are described in this ballad, with a mood somewhere between humor and grim realism. (FAC II 133: from "Songs o' th' Cowboys" corralled by Chuck Haas.)

Thar's no respect fer youth er age
   A-board the Californy Stage:
Yu pull an' haul an' push an' yank
   Ontill ye're ga'nted lean an' lank.
They crowd you in with Chinese men,
   Like fat hawgs packed into a pen;
They're bound your stomick to provoke
   With musty plug-terbacker smoke.

Oh, they started this dam thievin' line
   Back in th' days o' Forty-Nine:
All peace an' comfort they defy;
   You pay, then ride "Root hawg er die!"

The ladies is compelled to sit
   With dresses in terbacker spit.
The gold-crazed men don't seem to care;
   Just talk an' lie, an' sing an' swear.
The dust lays deep in summertime,
   The mountains steep an' hard to climb;
The drivers yell, "Whoa, Moll! Whoa, Bill!
   Climb out, all hands, an' push up hill!"

When them dam drivers feel inclined
  They make you walk along behind,
An' on your shoulders lug a pole
  To help 'em through some big mud-hole.
They smile an' promise, when you pay,
  "You'll have to walk 'bout half the way!"
Them lying skunks kin dam well laugh . . .
  You have to push the other half!

Thar's no respect fer youth er age
  A-board the Californy Stage!
You pull an' haul, an' cuss the day
  You left a good home fur away:
An' when at last, all pale an' sore,
  You reach the Sacremento's shore,
You're too dam heartsick fer to scold,
  And too dam weak to pick up gold!

59a. *Humbug Steamship Companies*

(John A. Stone, *Put's Original California Songster.* San Francisco: Appleton & Co., 1855. Pp. 43–44.)

The greatest imposition that the public ever saw,
Are the California steamships that run to Panama;
They're a perfect set of robbers, and accomplish their designs
By a gen'ral invitation of the people to the mines.

    Then come along, come along, you that want to go,
    The best accommodations, and the passage very low;
    Our boats they are large enough, don't be afraid,
    The *Golden Gate* is going down to beat the *Yankee Blade.*
    Then come along, don't be afraid,
    The *Golden Gate* is going down to beat the *Yankee Blade.*

They have opposition on the route, with cabins very nice,
And advertise to take you for half the usual price;
They get thousands from the mountains, and then deny their bills,
So you have to pay the prices, or go back into the hills.

When you start from San Francisco, they treat you like a dog,
The victuals you're compell'd to eat ain't fit to feed a hog;
And a drunken mate a cursing and damning you around,
And wishing that the boat would sink and every one be drowned.

The captain goes to dinner and begins to curse the waiter,
Knocks him out of hearing with a thundering big potato;
The cabin maid, half crazy, breaks the meat dish all to smash,
And the steward comes a running with a plate of mouldy hash.

You are driven round the steerage like a drove of hungry swine,
And kicked ashore at Panama by the Independent Line;
Your baggage is thrown overboard, the like you never saw,
A trip or two will sicken you of going to Panama.

60. *On the Road to Cook's Peak*

Mule-drawn wagons, pulled by from one to ten span, were a common
sight in the Great Basin and Southwest to the time of their eventual
displacement by the Model T Ford. (FAC II 668: Miscellaneous texts,
Archive of Folk Song, Library of Congress.)

If you'll listen a while I'll sing you a song
And as it is short it won't take me long,
There are some things of which I will speak
Concerning the stage on the road to Cook's Peak.

    On the road to Cook's Peak,
    On the road to Cook's Peak,
    Concerning the stage on the road to Cook's Peak.

'Twas in the morning at eight forty-five,
I was hookin' up all ready to drive
Out where the miners for minerals seek
With two little mules on the road to Cook's Peak.

With my two little mules I jog along
And try to cheer them with ditty and song,
O'er the wild prairie where coyotes sneak
While driving the stage on the road to Cook's Peak.

Sometimes I have to haul heavy freight
Then it is I get home very late,
In rain or shine, six days a week,
'Tis the same old mules on the road to Cook's Peak.

And when with the driving of stage I am through
I will to my little mules bid adieu
And hope that those creatures, so gentle and meek,
Will have a good friend on the road to Cook's Peak.

Now all kind friends that travel about,
Come take a trip on the Wallis Stage route,
With plenty of grit they never get weak,
Those two little mules on the road to Cook's Peak.

61. *Two-Gun Percy*

Stage robberies by mounted and armed bandits have become classic scenes in the "Western": fiction, radio, cinema, or TV. Here the holdup itself is followed by the bandits' capture of the lawmen out to apprehend them, and by their subsequent heroic rescue. By whom? Why, a half-pint stranger, ironically dubbed Two-Gun Percy, who turns out to be marshal in another frontier settlement. (PNFQ 485.)

We was waitin' a while for the evenin' stage,
    When a little stranger blows into town.
He looks about eighteen years of age,
    An' two big six-guns holds him down.

He 'lows that he's goin' to Painted Staff,
    In a voice like a woman — soft and clear.
An' Sheriff Bob, he says with a laugh,
    "We ought to keep Two-Gun Percy here."

Just then the stage comes a-rollin' in,
    An' we see at once that there's something wrong.
Buck Jenks, the driver, has lost his grin,
    An' the Fargo messenger ain't along.

Then Buck says, "Sheriff, the stage was stopped
    By the Black Hill gang, who have broke from jail.
Bat Barnes, the Fargo man, was dropped,
    An' they got his box an' all the mail.

As the sheriff sends for his hoss an' mine,
    Buck tells it was done in Indian Vale.
An' we gallop back, along the line,
    While a posse is formin' to take the trail.

An' as we git near the holdup ground,
    We are watchin' the road for any tracks,
When, suddenly, without a sound,
    We are roped right off'n our hosses' backs.

The bandits has ketched us both asleep,
    An' they tie us up, with a picket rope.
Then we watch them wait, where the shade is deep,
    As the little stranger comes up the slope.

An' we watch the loop as the rope is swung,
    Then Sheriff Bob gives a warnin' cry,
An' the small man ducks when the rope is flung,
    An' we sees the noose go whizzin' by.

Then a big gun shines in each small hand,
    An' the deep woods echoes the six-gun's crack,
As he shoots his way through the robber band,
    An' he leaves them dead, in his pony's track.

Then he cuts us loose with a funny laugh,
    An' he says, "Well, Sheriff, it's comin' dark,
An' I got to be gittin' to Painted Staff.
    I'm marshal there, an' my name is Clark."

62. *Boliver Riggin*

This prospector's sad odyssey is served to us in the rhythms of a limerick—a note of sophistication. (FAC II 706: William L. Alderson papers, University of Oregon.)

> There was an old man in the county of Pike
> And his name was Boliver Riggin,
> And like an old fool
> He bought an old mule
> And vanished the ranch for the diggin's.
>
> Bolly traveled on through the mire and the mud
> Till he came to the North Platte River,
> There he put in
> But the mule couldn't swim
> So away went his bacon forever.

63. *Black Bart*

The line between melodrama and plain "corn" is a fine one: Black Bart had visited Hollywood before this bit of doggerel was dripped off the pen of some aspiring script writer. (Hendren 464: manuscript.)

Black Bart held up the Cow Creek stage in his manner so polite:
"Ladies and gentlemen," he said, "be pleased now to alight.

"Your money and your jewelry I'm aimin' to collect,
To aid a worthy purpose that I trust you will respect."

They lined up with their hands high and Bart he passed the hat.
They filled it and he grinned at 'em for he was standing pat.

The driver was a brave man, too gallant for his health,
And he had swore that with his life he'd guard the express wealth.

He tried to draw his peg leg but Black Bart saw the move,
He shot the driver through the head, his marksmanship to prove.

He spoke to all the passengers, "Now take it in good part.
It's really quite an honor to be held up by Black Bart."

64. *The Cow Girl*

The stereotyped fights between cowboys and Indians which infest all "western" creations of the mass media are based on an abundance of actual conflict such as is presented in this powerful specimen of frontier realism. Cowboys frequently delivered beef on the hoof to military outposts of the West. (FAC II 607: Archive of Folk Song, Library of Congress, No. 1482A2. Recorded by Alan and Elizabeth Lomax, sung by Howard Spurlock, Clay County, Kentucky, 1937.)

A pretty fair maiden all out on the plains,
Who helped me herd cattle through hail storm, and rains,

She helped me herd cattle whatever were done,
She'd drink her corn whiskey from the cold bitter cup,

She'd drink her corn whiskey and swing her lasso,
As fine as a lily, as white as the snow.

We camped in the canyon in the fall of the year,
To feed Uncle Sam's soldiers a herd of fat steers.

I taught her the language of a cowboy's command,
To hold her six-shooter in each little hand;

To hold a six-shooter and never to run,
As long as a bullet was left in her gun.

The Indians broke over us one dark stormy night,
Sprang from the valley, sprang out for a fight;

Sprang from the valley with a gun in each hand,
"Come all you brave cowboys, let's save our dear land."

It thundered, it lightninged and down fell the rain,
Along came a bullet and dashed out her brains.

I left her layin' in a furrin land,
And how I done it I can't understand.

In a grave that I dug out way in the West
The cow girl sleeps in the home of the blest.

65. *Waring of Sonoratown*

Craftsmanship and nonchalance are always admired, even if it is a matter of gun-play and murder. The author is Henry Herbert Knibbs. (*Songs of the Trail.* Boston: Houghton Mifflin Co., 1920. Pp. 49–50. Copyright 1948 by Ida Julia Knibbs. Reprinted by permission of the publisher, Houghton Mifflin Company.)

The heat acrost the desert was a-swimmin' in the sun,
   When Waring of Sonora-town,
   Jim Waring of Sonora-town,
From Salvador come ridin' down, a-rollin' of his gun.

He was singin' low an' easy to his pony's steady feet,
   But his eye was live an' driftin'
   Round the scenery an' siftin'
All the crawlin' shadows shiftin' in the tremblin' gray mesquite.

Eyes was watchin' from a hollow where a outlaw Chola lay:
   Two black, snaky eyes, a-yearnin'
   For Jim's hoss to make the turnin',
Then—to loose a bullet burnin' through his back—the Chola way.

Jim Waring's gaze, a-rovin' free an' easy as he rode,
   Settled quick—without him seemin'
   To get wise an' quit his dreamin'—
On a shiny ring a-gleamin' where no ring had ever growed.

But the lightnin' don't give warnin'—just a lick, an' she is through.
   Waring set his gun to smokin',
   Playful-like—like he was jokin',
An'—a Chola lay a-chokin', an' a buzzard cut the blue.

66. *Two Ponies Shy*

Bandits hold up a mine, kill two tenderfeet, and steal their clothes for disguise. They kill a guard while robbing a Wells Fargo stage, but are apprehended and shot when the stolen ponies bolt, leaving them stranded right on main street. Ho, hum! Just a normal day in a western town! (PNFQ 486.)

Three-finger Dan an' Soapy Sam hold up the Eagle mine;
An' then they meet two tenderfeet as they head for the borderline.

They strip the tenderfeet of their duds, an' even take their boots.
An' when that's done, Dan pulls a gun an' kills the poor galoots.

They ride hard thirty miles or more, an' then they stop their flight,
In a high ravine near Aberdeen just as it's gettin' night.

An' then they stretch them out to sleep 'til somewhere 'long
        'bout ten,
An' after they rest, they both get dressed in the clothes of the
        two dead men.

They cinch the saddles an' hide their packs, then lead the
        ponies down,
An' leave them untied, an' ready to ride in the middle of the town.

Three-finger Dan an' Soapy Sam feel safe in their fancy dress,
So they lean on a rail by the moonlit trail an' wait for the
        night express.

The ol' stage rattles up the hill, pulled by the tired nags,
It stops near Dan, while the Fargo man hauls out the money bags.

Sam's two shots drill the Fargo guard, Dan yanks the bags from
        his hand,
Each waves a gun, as they turn an' run to the place where the
        ponies stand.

But the strange clothes make the ponies bolt, knockin' the
        robbers down,
Then the office guard starts shootin' hard an' wakes the whole
        durned town.

The six-guns roar from every door at the two in the moon's
        bright light,
Sam drops his gun, then Dan is done. They have lost their last
        big fight.

67. *Ballad of the Broomtails*

The style in this ballad of range warfare is packed with concentrated energy like an all-purpose vitamin pill. Hamill, a legitimate rancher, and his two sons accost four horse thieves at their camp, ask them to skedaddle and leave the stolen cavvy behind. In the ensuing fight not one of the seven survive—a fact which leaves us perplexed as to how the tale itself came through! (Hendren 3: manuscript.)

Powder Face and Jerry Horn, Smoky Sims and Tandy
   Stole a bunch of horses from the O-Bar-O,
Headed for the high grass across the Rio Grande,
   Camped on Thunder Mountain where the tall trees grow.

Hamill and his two sons, Thunder Mountain riders,
   Saw the bunch of broomtails, read the valley brand,
Told the valley horse thieves they didn't like outsiders
   Grazing any horses on the Mountain land.

Powder Face and Tandy were loaded with excuses.
   "Grazin' in your front yard? Hell! Ya got us wrong!"
"Yes," said Jerry Horn, "these are stray cayuses
   And we were just wonderin' where the bunch belongs."

"So," said Judson Hamill, "then that will save you trouble.
   You can leave the broomtails grazing where they are."
Smoky shook the skillet and the grease began to bubble,
   Tandy looked at Hamill and his look went far.

"Mebbe so," said Powder Face, "you're askin' us to ramble."
   Smoky set the skillet down and stood up slow.
"Mebbe so," said Tandy, "you'd like a little gamble.
   High cards settle where the broomtails go."

"Cut," said Smoky Sims, "we got nothin' else but aces."
   "Aces," said Jerry Horn, and he drew his gun.
The air was full of white smoke flashing in their faces
   And Jerry Horn lay twisting in the high hot sun.

Smoky took a soft slug a span below the shoulder,
   Leaned against a tall tree and dropped his man.
Powder Face and Tandy crouched behind a boulder,
   Kept a burning powder while the red blood ran

Continued

The last of Hamill's boys fell as Tandy's rifle chattered,
  A bullet whispered "Powder Face," and he fell dead.
As Smoky coughed his life out the stolen horses scattered,
  Tandy looked at Hamill and his laugh broke red.

Both sons gone, Hamill's eyes began to wander;
  He tried to raise his rifle but his hand spread wide.
Tandy laughed, 'We'll take the tally yonder,
  Across the Hump to yonder where the dead men ride!

"Bacon's curled" — he eyed the smoking skillet —
  "Broomtails scattered and I'm damn near done.
Hand looked good — drew — but couldn't fill it."
  And he lay stark staring in the high hot sun.

68. *The Trail Herd*

These unpretentious lyrics ring true to the setting and mood of the trail drive crews. The language and preoccupations are authentic and appropriate: there were occasional poetic, almost tender, moments for the trail drivers, despite their basic commitment to the play of brawn and muscle. (Hendren 439: manuscript.)

Clouded sun on coolin' morn,
  Squeakin' taps and spurs a-rattle,
Loungin' 'cross my saddle horn,
  Trailin' dull-eyed bawlin' cattle.
Chokin' dust clouds in the air,
  Off across the range a-driftin',
Punchers cussin' stragglers there
  As the mornin' mist is liftin'.

Wild-eyed mavericks on the prod,
  Plungin' ponies, buckin', snortin',
On across the sun baked sod
  Full o' ginger, a-cavortin'.
Ol' chuck wagon on ahead
  Fer to get the grub pile ready,
Sun a-blazin' fiery red,
  Calves a-wobblin' or unsteady.

Summer day a-growin' old
  As the crimson sun is sinkin',
River sparklin' just like gold
  Where the thirsty herd is drinkin'.
Cook a-yellin', "Grub pile, boys!"
  Cups on ol' tin plates a-rattle,
Punchers makin' lots o' noise
  On the bed ground with the cattle.

Continued

Silence on the midnight air,
　Me on night herd slowly moggin'
Round the bedded cattle there,
　Singin' to 'em as I'm joggin'.
Camp fire twinklin' down below,
　River sort o' lullabyin'
To the sleepers soft an' low
　On their blanket beds a-lyin'.

Second watch a-rollin' out,
　Sleepy-eyed with grimy faces,
At the foreman's lusty shout,
　Saddlin' up to take our places.
Me a-drowsin' off to rest
　With the starry sky above me,
Thoughts of you within my breast,
　Dreamin', dreamin' that you love me.

69. *The Poor Lonesome Cowboy*

Night herding was a time for meditation and for slow rhythms to match the steady walk of a sure-footed horse. This song was a favorite, and sometimes was sung with a few stanzas in Spanish. (FAC I 515: English text sung by Kathy Dagel, Kansas, 1959; FAC I 470: Spanish text sung by Jack Humphrey, Arizona, 1963.)

I ain't got no father, I ain't got no father,
I ain't got no father, to buy the clothes I wear.

I ain't got no mother, I ain't got no mother,
I ain't got no mother, to mend the clothes I wear.

I ain't got no sister, I ain't got no sister,
I ain't got no sister to come and play with me.

I ain't got no brother, I ain't got no brother,
I ain't got no brother to drive the steers with me.

I ain't got no sweetheart, I ain't got no sweetheart,
I ain't got no sweetheart, to sing and talk with me.

I'm a poor lonesome cowboy, I'm a poor lonesome cowboy,
I'm a poor lonesome cowboy and a long way from home.

Yo no tengo dinero, yo no tengo papel,
Yo no tengo dinero, now ain't that hell!

Yo tengo dinero, yo tengo papel,
Yo tengo mujer, now ain't that swell!*

---

*I've no money . . . I've no cigarette paper . . . .
I've money . . . I've paper . . . a woman . . .

70. *The Philosophical Cowboy*

This poem gives an honest, good-humored view of a cowboy's life on the open range. The refrain and accompanying melody have floated down through every episode in our history since the Revolution. The author signed himself "J. H. S." (*Out West,* April 1911, p. 336.)

On the Double Circle Range where the grass grows green
The cattle get wild and broncs get mean,
And the calves get bigger as the days go by,
So we got to keep a-rimming, boys, it's root hog or die.

If you ride 'em out of horses you've got to keep them shod,
If you can't shoe them standing then lay them on the sod.
You can tack the iron on them if you're a mind to try,
So get busy, boys, for it's root hog or die.

In the morning after breakfast about daylight
Throw your saddle on a horse and pull your cinches tight,
Your bronc may jump crooked or he may jump high,
But we all got to ride them, boys, it's root hog or die.

Oh the hills are rough and rocky but we got to make the drive,
When you start a bunch of cattle you better come alive,
If you ever get a maverick you must get him on the fly,
So you better take to them, boys, it's root hog or die.

When the long day is over you'll be glad to see the chef
With a pot of black coffee and another'n full of beef,
And some sourdough biscuits to take the place of pie,
When he hollers, "Come and git it," it's root hog or die.

In the middle of the night it is sometimes awful hard
To leave your warm blankets when you're called on guard,
And pass the weary moments while the stars are in the sky
Humming to the cattle, boys, it's root hog or die.

Sometimes it's dreadful stormy and sometimes it's pretty clear,
You may work a month and you might work a year,
But you can make a winning if you'll come alive and try,
For the whole world over, boys, it's root hog or die.

71. On the Trail from a Puncher's Point of View

Here we have some of the principal episodes of a trail drive told with realism and underlying good humor, despite the adversities of weather and cattle, and even the pleasures and sundry fauna at the trail's-end city. Broke within a few days after the drive is ended, the cowboy will take it in stride, returning to the range by stealing a ride on a west-bound train. (Gordon-Oregon 170: manuscript.)

So early in the morning before the break of day
You'll hear the cook a hollering, "Turn out there, chuck-a-way!"
You'll tumble out of your suggans with many a growl-cuss-word
And rope a bucking bronco and be off to join the herd.

You follow up the cattle for many a dreary mile,
The wind a constant blowing and the dust as thick as 'ile,
A steady churn of alkali that fills your eyes and nose,
And perhaps a sullin' dogie to round up your other woes.

You're spitting dimes from dryness, your tobacco don't taste right,
You strain your eyes to bursting but no water hole's in sight,
Then you curse the boss for traveling such a doggoned thirsty trail,
You know a hundred better, he's not fit to drive a nail.

At night, you've just fell over when someone pulls your tarp:
"Get up! You're next guard," he shouts, "I've called you twice,
        look sharp!"
There ain't no use of your roaring, but you can do it by the yard
For you have to crawl your night horse and stand your two
        hours' guard.

Some nights it's not so tough, when the moon is shining clear
And the cattle is quietly sleeping, to the biggest meanest steer;
Then you circle around the bed ground to an old time
        puncher's song,
And your two hours of watching don't seem one-half so long.

But when the thunders bellow and the rain's a solid sheet,
And your horse for wind and mudholes can scarcely keep his feet,
And the cattle keep a milling as if they would never tire,
And the lightnings playing continually on their horns in points
        of fire,

Continued

The flashes run together as if they would never stop,
And you see as plain as daylight the steer next to you drop,
Then, boys, just tar and feather me and ride me on a rail
If you ever catch me venturing on another cattle trail.

But that's all soon forgotten when you reach your journey's goal
And the cattle has been delivered and you get your little roll.
Then you start out on a bender and you paint the city red,
And you're lucky in the morning if you find yourself in bed.

You keep it up a little while, your big roll going fast,
For with dance halls and bad whiskey, the biggest roll can't last,
And very soon you're rocky with a bad case of the shakes,
Your choice—between a box car, blind, baggage, or the brakes.

72. *Passing of the Wrangler*

A number of "western" clichés are concentrated in this ballad: nature as a malign adversary to man; a subtle intermingling of range realism and cowcamp schmaltz; glimpses of the cowboy's code (a proper burial, momism, deeds above talk, rough range "lingo," a vapid but undeniable Christian faith). The author is said to be Henry C. Fellow. (PNFQ 354.)

"Wrangle up yer broncs, Bill,
　　Let us hit the trail;
Cinch 'em up a knot er two,
　　'Fore there comes a gale.

"Fill the wagon full o' chuck,
　　'Fore we cut adrift;
Fer we'll have a time, Bill,
　　With this winter shift.

"My bones, they feel a blizzard
　　A-hatchin' in the West,
An' I must load my gizzard
　　With some pizen piker's best.

"Sam, git yer chips together,
　　An' stack 'em in a box;
An' gather up the tether
　　Ropes, shirts, and dirty socks;

"An' lash 'em to the cayuse
　　An' strap 'em tight an' strong,
Fer we're goin' to have to ride, Sam,
　　Kase it seems they's somethin' wrong.

"Pards, see the clouds a-shiftin';
　　They's goin' to turn a trick
An' make us go a-driftin',
　　Afore we reach the crick.

"It's a hundred miles, ye know, boys,
　　To reach the O-X camp,
An' we'll have to keep a'rollin',
　　Er we'll ketch a frosty cramp.

Continued

151

"So skin the mules aplenty
    With yer double-triggered crack;
An' keep the broncs a-goin'
    Jist so ye know the track!"

So with a whoop an' holler,
    The rounders, full o' pluck—
An' tanked up to the collar—
    With their wagonload of chuck,

They left the Dodge behind 'em
    An' started fer the south;
With the wind a-blowin'
    A peck o' dirt a mouth.

They sca'ce could see the other
    Feller, lopin' through the cloud;
Or hear nothin' but the thunder,
    An' the flappin' o' their shroud!

Tumble weeds a-rollin'
    With a forty-minute clip,
An' the clouds a-pilin'
    Up like a phantom ship.

With 'er double-triggered action,
    The wind she turned her tail,
An' kicked out all the suction
    Fer the souther's gale.

She started in to rainin'
    An' follered with a sleet;
An' kept 'er speed a-gainin',
    A-throwin' down 'er sheet,

Till everything was covered,
    A frozen glare of ice.
Yet she still closter hovered,
    An' pinched us like a vise.

That blizzard come a-peltin'
    With 'er frozen shot;
An' sich snow a-driftin'
    I never have forgot!

We couldn't see a nothin'
   Nor hear a rounder croak,
But the gurgle o' the pizen
   A-puttin' us to soak.

We kept the hosses movin'
   From bein' froze to death;
While waitin' fer the mornin'
   To thaw us with his breath.

But when the snowy mornin'
   Had come in with his smile,
He'd left a ghastly warnin'
   Fer many and many a mile.

A thousand head o' cattle
   Caught driftin' in the storm,
Were frozen, while a-millin',
   A-tryin' to keep warm.

Poor Sammy, with the wagon,
   Was found a mile alone,
Was stuck adrift, an' frozen,
   An' harder'n a stone.

Ol' Bill, he froze his fingers,
   An' blistered up his face,
Tryin' to pitch his ringers
   An' a-fightin' fer the ace.

I fell into a canyon,
   With my cayuse an' my traps,
An' shuffled for the joker,
   With the cinchin' straps.

I warmed myself aplenty
   A-keepin' up the fight,
A-skinnin' ol' McGinty
   Till a-comin' o' the light.

Poor Sam! He boozed aplenty
   To stack him in a heap;
An' the devils swiped his ante
   When he went to sleep.

Continued

153

So Bill and me together
  Stood in silence by the wag—
On, not a-knowin' whether
  To swig another jag,

Or cut the cussed pizen
  That had foggled up our breath,
An' kept our spirits risin',
  Without a fling o' death.

So me an' Bill, we tackled
  The job without a drop,
An' in the hill we hackled
  A grave with an icy top.

An' shuffled Sammy in it,
  An' banked him with snow,
An' 'rected up a monument
  To let the nesters know.

We had done our solemn dooty,
  An' planted him in style,
With the whitest snow o' heaven
  Heaped on him in a pile.

Poor Bill! he sniffled a little
  When I lifted up my hat,
An' let some weepin' splatter
  On Sammy's frozen mat.

Sam wa'n't no idle rustler,
  No one could ride the range
Better'n he, nor brand 'em,
  Nor dip 'em fer the mange.

His check book showed a balance,
  Fer a wrangler o' the stuff,
Fer a-helpin' of his mother,
  No one could speak enough.

His heart was where God put it,
  His blood was always red;
His mouth he alluz shut it,
  When troubles was ahead.

An' if the storm was ragin',
  He rode the line alone,
An' never once a-stagin'
  Some other's stunt his own.

Fer his larnin' he was known,
  Figgered with the letter X;
Never had to once be shown,
  Was a mangy maverick's.

Set an' count a herd o' stars
  Driftin' from the hand o' God;
Tell us all about the flowers
  Playin' bopeep in the sod.

Hope the judge will let us through
  When he rounds up at the gate;
But, ol' pard, I'm fearin', though,
  Sam'll be a little late.

Peace be then to Sammy's ashes,
  Till the round-up o' the race,
When each wrangler's checkbook cashes
  What it's worth an' at its face.

73. *Night Herding Songs*

Night herding songs are as close to a distinctive literary form as any-
thing to be encountered in cowboy and western verse. They are a kind
of lullaby to soothe animals on the bed ground, and perhaps even more
to soothe the nerves of the cowboys assigned to night guard. Three
texts of a favorite night herding song are given here to suggest to the
readers how verse evolves when it is taken over by the folk. There is
internal evidence to suggest origin of the song in an ancient Irish
lullaby.

A. RUN LITTLE DOGIES
    (Archive of Folk Song, Library of Congress No.
    1849A1, B1, 2. Recorded by John Lomax from
    the singing of Francis Sullivan, Washington, D.C.)

>   As I looked out of my window
>   I saw a cowboy come riding along,
>   His hat was shoved back and his spurs kept a-jingling
>   And as he drew near he was singing this song.
>
>   Hush, ciaola, little baby lie easy,
>   Who's your real father may never be known.
>   Oh, it's weeping, wailing, rocking the cradle,
>   And tending a baby that's none of your own.
>
>   When spring comes along we round up the dogies,
>   We stick on their brands and we bob off their tails,
>   Pick out the strays, then the herd is inspected,
>   And then next day we go on the trail.
>
>   Singing whoop pi-o-whoop, run along little dogies,
>   For Montana will be your new home.
>   Oh, it's whooping, swearing, driving the dogies,
>   It's our misfortune we ever did roam.
>
>   Oh, it's worst in the night just after a round-up
>   When dogies are grazing from the herd all around.
>   You have no idea of the trouble they give us
>   To the cowboys who are holding them on the bed ground.
>
>   Whoop pi-o-whoop, run along you little dogies,
>   For Montana will be your new home.
>   Oh, it's whooping, swearing, driving the dogies,
>   It's our misfortune we ever did roam.

Oh, some think we go on trail for pleasure,
  But I can tell them that they are dead wrong,
If I ever got any fun out of trailing
  I'd have no reason for singing my song.

    Hush, ciaola, little baby lie easy,
    Who's your real father may never be known.
    Oh, it's weeping, wailing, rocking the cradle,
    And tending a baby that's none of your own.

B. AS I WALKED OUT
  (FAC II 682: from the Owen Wister Journals,
  University of Wyoming, 1893, pp. 41–42.)

    As I walked out one morning for pleasure
      I met a cowpuncher a jogging along
    His hat was thrown back and his spurs was a jingling
      And as he advanced he was singing this song.

      Sing hooplio, get along my little dogies
      For Wyoming shall be your new home,
      It's hooping and yelling and cursing those dogies
      To our misfortune but none of your own.

    In the springtime we round up the dogies,
      Slap on the brands and bob off their tails,
    Then we cut and the herd is inspected
      And then we throw them onto the trail.

    In the evening we round in the dogies
      As they are grazing from herd all around,
    You have no idee the trouble they give us
      As we are holding them on the bedground.

    In the morning we throw off the bedground
      Aiming to graze them an hour or two,
    When they are full you think you can drive them
      On the trail, but be damned if you do.

    Some fellows go on the trail for pleasure
      But they have got this thing down wrong,
    If it hadn't been for these troublesome dogies,
      I never would thought of writing this song.

C. GIT ALONG LITTLE DOGIES
(FAC II 133: from "Songs o' th' Cowboys," cor-
ralled by Chuck Haas.)

As I was a-walkin', one mornin' for pleasure,
    I spied a young cowboy a-lopin' along:
His hat was throw'd back, and his spurs was a-jingle,
    And as he rid by he was singin' this song.

    Tip-pee ti-yi-yo, git along little dogies;
    It's your misfortune and none o' my own,
    Yip-pee ti-yi-yo, git along little dogies,
    The plains o' Wyoming will be your new home.

First thing in the spring we round-up all the dogies;
    We ear-mark, and brand 'em, and bob off their tails;
Then wrangle our hosses, load up the chuck wagon,
    And throw the wild snuffy bunch on the North trail.

Some boys ride the long North trail just for the pleasure,
    But soon find they figgered most terrible wrong;
Them dogies are kinky, and try for to scatter
    All over the plains, as we roll 'em along.

    It's whoo-pee, and yip-pee, whilest drivin' the dogies;
    Oh how I wish that they'd ramble alone.
    It's punchin', and yippin', "Git on little dogies,"
    For you know Wyoming will soon be your home.

Your maws was all raised-up away down in Texas,
    Whar sandburrs, and cacti, and jimpson-weed grow.
We'll fill you on prick'y-pear, catclaw, and *cholla*,
    Then roll you along the trail for Idaho.

Oh, you'll soon be soup for ol' Uncle Sam's Injuns,
    It's "Beef, heap good beef," I hear 'em all cry.
So git along, ramble on, roll little dogies,
    You'll all be beef-stew in the sweet by and by.

74. *The Stampede*

This is the highly artistic and dramatic account of a cattle stampede. Western images abound: mounted hands frantically singing cowboy songs to forestall the inevitable; the jump of a wolf and the mad rush of the cattle; a doomed puncher shooting in the lead in a vain attempt to "get them milling;" and finally, the first two articles in the cowboy code—devotion to duty at risk of one's own life, and boyish attachment to the girl back home. Both form (i.e., stanzas of substantial length) and content have epic characteristics. The author is Freeman E. Miller. (*Songs from the Southwest Country*. New York: The Knickerbocker Press, 1898. Pp. 42–44.)

We took our turn at the guard that night, just Sourdough Charlie
     and I,
And as we mounted our ponies, there were clouds in the
     western sky;
And we knew that before the morning the storm, by the north
     wind stirred,
Would scourge the plains with its furies fierce and madden the
     savage herd;
But we did not shrink the danger; we had ridden the plains
     for years, —
The crash of the storm and the cattle's cry were music in our ears.

We drove the herd to a circle, for the winds were calm, and
     we knew
That somewhere near to the midnight shift the storm-fiends
     would be due.
We rode the rounds unceasingly, and we worked with an
     anxious will
Until the cattle were lying down and the mighty herd was still,
And only the musical breathing of the bedded beasts arose
As we rounded the living circle and guarded their light repose.

Then the storm came in in anger; the winds of a sudden turned,
The lightnings flamed through the seething skies, and the prairies
     blazed and burned;
The thunders rolled like an avalanche, and they shook the
     rocking world,
That trembling quaked as the storm so wild its banners of
     blaze unfurled;

Continued

The fires flew over the frightened herd and leaped from horn to horn
Till horrible clamors rose and fell in chaos of fear forlorn.

The herd awoke in a minute; but we rode through the flashing ways
And sang with a will the olden songs we learned in our
        childhood days;
The human voice has a wondrous power, and the wildest beast
        that moans
Forgets its fear in a dream of peace at the sound of its tender tones:
And on through the blinding flashes and on through the dark
        and the light,
We rode with the old songs ringing, and we prayed for the
        death of night.

I never could tell how it happened; there came a tremendous crash,
A wolf jumped out of the chaparral, — and the herd was off in
        a flash!
And Charlie was riding before them; then I saw him draw his gun
And fire at the plunging leaders, till he turned them one by one;
Then the darkness fell, — I could not see, — and then in the
        blinding light
My pard went down, and the maddened herd swept on through the
        savage night!

Him I found where the cattle rushed in the wild of their wandering,
Broken and beaten by scores of hoofs, a crushed and a
        mangled thing!
And his pony lay with a broken leg, as dead as a rotten log,
Where its foot had slipped in the hidden hole of a worthless
        prairie-dog.
We buried him there — you can see the stones — and whether we
        die or live,
We gave him the best of a funeral that a cowboy camp can give.

His name? It was Sourdough Charlie, sir; and whether a
        good or bad,
We called him that for a score of years — it was all the name
        he had!
I found a locket above his heart, with a picture there of grace
That showed a girl with a curly head and a most uncommon face;
Hero, you say? Well, maybe so; for I know it is oft confessed
That he's the kind of a man it takes for the work here in the West.

75. Kit Carson's Ride

Joaquin Miller's poem has the stamp of his particular genius; even the poetic form deviates from that of the folk. Still, it belongs in this particular anthology because of its epic characteristics and by its evocation of a panoply of the stereotyped images and situations of the frontier experience: the seduction of an Indian maid; flight on a horse she has stolen from her own father's *remuda*; the prairie fire and stampede of domestic and wild beasts before its fiendish onslaught. All these are components of the "Western" myth. (Our source for this item is PNFQ 238; both shorter and longer versions of the poem have appeared in anthologies of Miller's works.)

> We lay low in the grasses and sunburnt clover
> That spread on the ground like a great brown cover,
> Northward and southward and west and away,
> To the Brazos, to where our lodges lay,
> One broad and unbroken sea of brown,
> Awaiting the curtains of night to come down
> To cover us over and conceal our light,
> With my brown bride, won from an Indian town
> That lay in the rear the full ride of a night.
>
> We lay low in the grass on the broad plain levels,
> Old Revels and I, and my stolen bride;
> And the heavens of blue and the harvest of brown
> And beautiful clover were welded as one,
> To the right and the left, in the light of the sun.
> Forty full miles, if a foot, to ride,
> Forty full miles, if a foot, and the devils
> Or red Comanches are hot on the track
> When once they strike it. Let the sun go down
> Soon, very soon, muttered bearded old Revels,
> As he peered at the sun, lying low on his back,
> Holding fast to his lasso. Then he jerked at his steed,
> And he sprang to his feet and glanced swiftly around,
> And then dropped, as if shot, with his ear to the ground;
> Then again to his feet, and to me, to my bride,
> While his eyes were like fire, his face like a shroud,
> His form like a king, and his beard like a cloud,
> And his voice loud and shrill, as if blown from a reed—
> "Pull, pull in your lassos, and bridle to steed,

Continued

And speed you, if ever for life you would speed,
And ride for your lives, for your lives you must ride!
For the plain is aflame, the prairie on fire,
And feet of wild horses hard-flying before,
I hear like a sea breaking high on the shore,
While the buffalo come like a surge of the sea,
Driven far by the flame, driving fast on us three,
As a hurricane comes, crushing palms in his ire."

We drew in the lasso, seized saddle and rein,
Threw them on, cinched them on, cinched them over again,
And again drew the girth, cast aside the macheers,
Cut away tapaderos, loosed the sash from its fold,
Cast aside the catenas, red-spangled with gold,
And gold-mounted Colts, the companions of years,
Cast the silken serapes to the wind in a breath,
And so bared to the skin sprang all haste to the horse —
Turned head to the Brazos in a red race with death,
Turned head to the Brazos with a breath in the air
Blowing hot from a king leaving death in his course;
Turned head to the Brazos with a sound in the air
Like the rush of an army, and a flash in the eye
Of a red wall of fire reaching up to the sky,
Stretching fierce in pursuit of a black rolling sea,
Rushing fast upon us, as the wind sweeping free,
And afar from the desert blew hollow and hoarse.

Not a word, not a wail from a lip was let fall,
Not a kiss from my bride, not a look nor low call
Of love-notes or courage; but on o'er the plain
So steady and still, leaning low to the mane,
With the heel to the flank and the hand to the rein,
Rode we on, rode we three, rode we nose and gray nose,
Reaching long, breathing loud, as a creviced wind blows;
Yet we broke not a whisper, we breathed not a prayer,
There was work to be done, there was death in the air,
And the chance was as one to a thousand for all.

Gray to gray nose, and each steady mustang
Stretched neck and stretched nerve till the earth rang,
And the foam from the flank and the croup and the neck
Flew around like the spray on a storm-driven deck.
Twenty miles! . . . thirty miles . . . a dim distant speck . . .
Then a long reaching line, and the Brazos in sight,
And I rose in my seat with a shout of delight.

I stood in my stirrup and looked to my right—
But Revels was gone; I glanced by my shoulder
And saw his horse stagger; I saw his head drooping
Hard down on his breast, and his naked breast stooping
Low down to the mane, as so swifter and bolder
Ran reaching out for us the red-footed fire.
To right and to left the black buffalo came,
A terrible surf on a red sea of flame
Rushing on in the rear, reaching high, reaching higher,
And we rode neck to neck to a buffalo bull,
The monarch of millions, with shaggy mane full
Of smoke and of dust, and it shook with desire
Of battle, with rage and with bellowings loud
And unearthly, and up through its lowering cloud
Came the flush of his eyes like a half-hidden fire,
While his keen crooked horns, through the storm of his mane,
Like black lances lifted and lifted again;
And I looked but this once, for the fire licked through,
And he fell and was lost, as we rode two and two.

I looked to my left then—and nose, neck and shoulder
Sank slowly, sank surely, till back to my thighs,
And up through the black blowing veil of her hair
Did beam full in mine her two marvelous eyes,
With a longing and love, yet a look of despair
And of pity for me, as she felt the smoke fold her,
And flames reaching far for her glorious hair.
Her sinking steed faltered, his eager eyes fell
To and fro and unsteady, and all the neck's swell
Did subside and recede, and the nerves fell as dead.
Then she saw sturdy 'Pache still lorded his head,
With a look of delight; for nor courage nor pride
Nor naught but my bride, could have brought him to me,
For he was her father's, and at South Santa Fe
Had once won a whole herd, sweeping everything down
In a race where the world came to run for the crown.
And so when I won the true heart of my bride—
My neighbor's and deadliest enemy's child,
And child of the kingly war chief of his tribe—
She brought me this steed to the border the night
She met Revels and me in her perilous flight
From the lodge of the chief to the north Brazos side;
And said, so half guessing of ill as she smiled,
As if jesting, that I, and I only, should ride

Continued

The fleet-footed 'Pache, so if kin should pursue
I should surely escape without other ado
Then to ride without blood, to the North Brazos side,
And await her — and wait till the next hollow moon
Hung her horn in the palms, when surely and soon,
And swift she would join me, and all would be well
Without bloodshed or word. And now, as she fell
From the front, and went down in the ocean of fire,
The last that I saw was a look of delight
That I should escape — a love — a desire —
Yet never a word, not one look of appeal,
Lest I should hand, should stay hand or stay heel
One instant for her in my terrible flight.

Then the rushing of fire around me and under,
And the howling of beasts, and a sound as of thunder,
Beasts burning and blind and forced onward and over,
As the passionate flame reached around them and wove her
Red hands in their hair, and kissed hot till they died,
Till they died with a wild and desolate moan;
As a sea heart broken on the hard brown stone —
And into the Brazos — I rode all alone —
All alone, save only a horse long-limbed
And blind and bare and burnt to the skin.
Then, just as the terrible sea came in
And tumbled its thousand hot into the tide,
Till the tide blocked up and the swift stream brimmed
In eddies, we struck on the opposite side.

76. Doney Gal

Here we have the slow, meditative rhythms of a favorite night herding song expressing the moods and images of trail and range. Note how the unity of the man and his mount reaffirms hope and triumph against four of the horsemen of malign nature: rain and hail, sleet and snow. (FAC II 605: Archive of Folk Song, Library of Congress No. 3681. Recorded by John A. Lomax.)

Traveling up the lonesome trail
Where man and his horse seldom ever fail;
Rain and hail, sleet and snow,
Me and my Doney-gal a-bound to go.

Sogging along through fog and dew,
Wishing for sunny days and you;
Rain and hail, sleet and snow,
Me and my Doney-gal a-bound to go.

Over the prairies lean and brown,
On through the wastes where stands no town;
Rain and hail, sleet and snow,
Me and my Doney-gal a-bound to go.

Swimming the rivers across our way,
We fight on forward day end on day;
Rain and hail, sleet and snow,
Me and my Doney-gal a-bound to go.

Bedding the cattle, singing a song,
We ride the night-herd all night long;
Rain and hail, sleet and snow,
Me and my Doney-gal a-bound to go.

Continued

When the storm breaks on the quiet mead,
We follow the cattle on their wild stampede;
Rain and hail, sleet and snow,
Me and my Doney-gal a-bound to go.

Trailing the herd through mountains green,
We pen the cattle in Abilene.
Rain and hail, sleet and snow,
Me and my Doney-gal a-bound to go.

Round the camp-fire's flickering glow,
We sing the songs of long ago.
Rain and hail, sleet and snow,
Me and my Doney-gal a-bound to go.

77. *A Cowboy Dance*

In their bent for identity apart from the mellowed effeminate behavior of eastern "gentlemen," the first two generations of western men cultivated rough, masculine, uninhibited behavior patterns—a kind of protective coloration for their basic "momism." (PC-F 31, 32: quoted from *The Expositor,* Fresno, California, 1885, with authorship attributed to N. L. F. Bachman. Note that the text is almost identical to that in James Barton Adams, *Breezy Western Verse.* Denver: Post Printing Co., 1889. Pp. 103–4.)

Get your little sage-hens ready,
　Trot 'em out upon the floor.
Line up there you cusses. Steady!
　Lively now! One couple more.
Shorty, shed that old sombrero;
　Broncho, douse that cigarette.
Stop your cussin', Cassimero,
　'Fore the ladies. Now, all set.

S'lute your ladies. All together;
　Ladies opposite the same;
Hit the lumber with your leather,
　Balance all, and swing your dame.
Bunch the heifers in the middle,
　Circle stags, and do-see-do
Pay attention to the fiddle—
　Swing her round, an' on you go.

First four forward; back to places;
　Second feller, shuffle back.
Now you got it down to cases
　Swing 'em till their trotters crack.
Gents all right a heel-and-toeing—
　Swing 'em, kiss 'em if you can;
On to next and keep a-going
　Till you hit your pards again.

Continued

Gents to center, ladies round 'em;
  Form a basket; balance all.
Whirl your girls to where you found 'em,
  Promenade around the hall.
Balance to your pards and trot 'em
  Round the circle double quick.
Grab and kiss 'em while you got 'em,
  Hold 'em to it if they kick.

Ladies, left hand to your sonnies,
  Alaman, grand right and left.
Balance all, and swing your honeys,
  Pick 'em up and feel their heft.
Promenade like skeery cattle,
  Balance all an' swing your sweets;
Shake your spurs and make 'em rattle.
  Keno! Promenade to seats.

78. *Cowboy Dance Song* (No. 2)

John A. Lomax says he got this song from "a prairie schooner woman near Silver City, New Mexico, who claimed to have ridden fifty miles on one occasion to attend a cowboy dance." Elemental "western" values are expressed: preference for the local girls, anticipation of marriage and children. Dance songs of similar character were disseminated throughout western Europe in the twelfth century by ambulant minstrels. (JL 23.)

> My name is Sam and I don't give a damn,
> All boys give the fiddler a dram.
> Swing the girls and let 'em go,
> Rattle your hoofs and don't be slow.
>
> > Doodle doody-doo, doodle doody-dee,
> > It's faro, monte, crack-a-lou,
> > Grip their fins and trot 'em through,
> > Balance and all pass by,
> > Grab your partners on the fly.
>
> Some likes girls that's pretty in the face
> And some likes girls that's small round the waist
> But give me the girl with the chubby fat hand
> And a dimple in her cheek like a hole in a pan.
>
> She ranges on the Live Oak Branch,
> The prettiest heifer at the ranch
> With hazel eyes and golden hair,
> And try to steal her if you dare.
>
> Oh, I'm as happy as a king
> For we'll be married in the spring,
> When grasses come you bet you
> And we'll start us up a little brand.

79. *Cowboy Dance Call*

Here, the basic rhythmic component of the western square dance is a simple couplet: a caller with any imagination at all could make them up as he went along, thus the dance might go on indefinitely. (J. R. Craddock, "The Cowboy Dance." *Coffee in the Gourd.* Publications of Texas Folk-Lore Society, II, 1917. Pp. 34–35. Reprinted by permission of the Texas Folklore Society.)

Choose your partner, form a ring,
Figure eight, and double-L-swing.

First swing six, then swing eight,
Swing 'em like swinging on a gate.

Ducks in the river, going to the ford,
Coffee in a little rag, sugar in a gourd.

Swing 'em once and let 'em go,
All hands left and docey doe.

You swing me and I'll swing you
And we'll all go to heaven in the same old shoe.

Chase the possum, chase the coon,
Chase that pretty girl around the room.

How will you swap, how will you trade,
This pretty girl for that old maid.

Wave the ocean, wave the sea,
Wave the pretty girl back to me.

Swing your partners once in a while,
Swing them all in Indian style.

Rope the cow and kill the calf,
Swing your partner a round and a half.

Swing your partners before you trade,
Grab 'em back and promenade.

Grab your partner and sail away,
Hurry up, it's breaking day.

Swing 'em round and round and round,
Pockets full of rocks to weight 'em down.

There comes a girl I used to know,
Swing her once and let her go.

When you meet your partner pat her on the head,
If she don't like coffee give her corn bread.

Three little sisters all in a row,
Swing 'em once and let 'em go.

Old shoe sole is about wore out,
Grab a girl and walk about.

Swing 'em east and swing 'em west,
Swing the girl that you love best.

80. *When Bronco Jack Was Spliced*

The artistic primitivism of this poem is comparable to the burlesque literary forms of Europe from the sixteenth to the eighteenth centuries. Vocabulary, grammatical forms, synthetic "western" dialect and the situation itself all come together to form a hilarious mock-heroic episode resembling the best moments of *Tom Jones* or *Don Quixote*. Authorship is attributed to James Barton Adams. (PNFQ 502.)

I've read in novel books about the rosy god of love,
Afloatin' 'round on angel wings the same as them above,
An' orange flowers an' golden bliss an' sweet things that are said,
An' sweetly tinklin' weddin' bells that ring when folks is wed.
An' probably the city dudes may pull it off that way,
With all the blissful fol-de-rols, jest as the novels say,
But in the nuptial catalog we had no sich things as that
The night that Broncho Jack was spliced at Simpson's,
     up the Platte.

Ol' Bill, the jestice of the peace, announced in a skeery way
That he had never bumped against a matermony play,
An' if of any legal p'int they found his doin's short,
They had a right to take a 'peal up to a higher court.
He asked 'em then to kindly grab each other by the paw
An' swore 'em both to keep the peace, accordin' to the law,
To wear the matermony brand, an' shy away from strife,
An' ended by pronouncin' them as legal man and wife.

That fur the ceremony seemed to run as slick as grease,
An' then ol' Bill assumed the right as jestice of the peace
To kiss the bride in legal form, an' tried to make the play,
When Jack he smashed him on the nose in quite a suddent way.
'Twas natural that such a break should make his honor hot,
An' risin' up he threatened to divorce 'em on the spot.
But when the groom apologized for flying off so quick,
Bill fined him fur contempt o' court, an' let the marriage stick.

When we had shuck the couple's hands an' wished 'em many joys,
An' made the usual reference to future bouncin' boys,
The fiddler tuned his music box an' hollered out to us
To choose our pardners for the dance; then came another muss;
The cowboys came stampedin' up like steers from every side
Each one insistin' on the right of dancin' with the bride.
But Jack he told 'em one and all they wasn't in the swim,
Fur 'cordin' to all precedent that right belonged to him.

It's never been discovered yet what disappointed chap
Turned loose a fist an' started sich a comprehensive scrap,
An' I have been bewildered-like an' bothered ever sence,
Endeavorin' to recollect the subsequent events.
There wasn't an invited guest but packed a head away
That sort o' kep' his memory green for many an' many a day,
An' Jack himself was hammered in a manner that sufficed
To make him such a fright his wife was sorry they was spliced.

Allow me to reiterate what I remarked above,
'Bout readin' in the novel books 'bout rosy gods of love,
An' orange buds, an' Cupid kids, an' angels' fleecy wings,
An' sweetly soundin' marriage bells, an' sich enticin' things.
I reckon that the novel chaps put in the most they say,
Because it tickles boys an' gals that's feelin' that-a-way —
Leastwise there was a scarcity of all sich things as that
That night that Broncho Jack was spliced at Simpson's,
        up the Platte.

81. *Buckskin Sam's Tribute to Texas Jack*

Here we have a folk elegy packed full of cowboy and western images.
Death on the prairies had its own special poignancy derived from the
bleakness of the landscape and the final severance of ties with kinfolk.
(PNFQ 41.)

No more will he turn the wild stampede,
With whoop and yell on the galloping steed,
No more take the red man's moccasined track,
'Mid bowstrings' twang and rifle crack.

No more with rare skill will his lasso twirl,
Or through the air his dreaded bowie hurl,
No more be poised on the mustang's back,
And drive wild herds on the Northern track.

No more the black snake deftly swing,
No more the *llanos* with his rifle ring,
The far-away trails his feet have trod
Will know him no more; he has gone to God.

Lay him to rest in his narrow home,
Beneath the sky, earth's natural dome,
Where southern virtue luxuriant grows,
Ne'er withered by icy northern snows.

There 'neath the Spanish moss and pine,
Where myriads of flowering creepers twine,
Let him repose in nature's wild,
Fit resting place for Nature's child.

There would I dig in grassy bank,
Far away from noisy cowbell's clank,
Where oft the red man leaves his track,
A fitting grave for Texas Jack.

There would I lay him down to rest,
Amid the scenes that he loved best,
I'd dig his lone grave long and wide,
And lay his rifle by his side.
I'd coil his lariat 'round his feet,
His serape use for a winding sheet.

But be his grave in the wildwood made,
Or in the city's busy mart,
Engrave on the stone in words of gold,
"There lies a noble heart."

82. *Across the Range*

The touching moments that precede death are enriched here with metaphors that reaffirm, in a language cowboys understand, the transcendence of the soul beyond the grave. (Hendren 43: manuscript.)

We brought him in with heavy feet,
    And eased him down from eye to eye,
Though no one spake, there passed the fear
    That Tom might die.

    Half sleeping, by the fire I sit,
    I awake and start, it is so strange
    To find myself alone,
    And Tom across the range.

He rallied when the sun was low, and spoke,
    I thought the words were strange,
"It's almost night, and I must go
    Across the range."

"What, Tom?" He smiled and added:
    "Yes, they've struck it rich there;
Jim, you know the parson told us,
    You'll come soon. Now Tom must go."

I brought his sweetheart's pictured face,
    Again that smile, as sad and strange,
"Tell her," he said, "that Tom has gone,
    Across the range."

The last light lingered on the hill,
    "There's a pass somewhere," then he said,
And lips and hands and eyes were still,
    And Tom was dead.

Part Four

Code of the Cowboy

PART IV

Code of the Cowboy

83. *The Ballad of Billy the Kid*

This ballad of stark realism and substantial biographical significance carries so many of the classic cowboy and western clichés that we give it here as a kind of summation. An outlaw-hero, an underdog, a loner, set adrift at age fourteen by a man's insult to his mother, a cardsharp with a Mexican sweetheart, he becomes the fearless and self-appointed avenger of wrongs, leads the lawmen on a long and bitter chase until at last he is shot down by a man "who once was his friend." The author is Henry Herbert Knibbs. (*Songs of the Lost Frontier.* Boston and New York: Houghton Mifflin Co., 1930. Pp. 34–37. Copyright 1958 by Ida Julia Knibbs. Reprinted by permission of the publisher, Houghton Mifflin Company.)

No man in the West ever won such renown
As young Billy Bonney of Santa Fe town,
And of all the wild outlaws that met a bad end,
None so quick with a pistol or true to a friend.

It was in Silver City his first trouble came,
A man called Billy's mother a very foul name;
Billy swore to get even, his chance it came soon,
When he stabbed that young man in Joe Dyer's saloon.

He kissed his poor mother and fled from the scene,
A bold desperado and not yet fifteen;
He hid in a sheep-camp but short was his stay,
For he stole an old pony and rode far away.

At monte and faro he next took a hand,
And lived in Tucson on the fat of the land;
But the game was too easy, the life was too slow,
So he drifted alone into Old Mexico.

It was not very long before Billy came back,
With a notch in his gun and some gold in a sack;
He struck for the Pecos his comrades to see,
And they all rode to Lincoln and went on a spree.

There he met his friend Tunstall and hired as a hand
To fight with the braves of the Jingle-Bob brand;
Then Tunstall was murdered and left in his gore;
To avenge that foul murder Young Billy he swore.

Continued

179

First Morton and Baker he swiftly did kill,
Then he slaughtered Bill Roberts at Blazer's sawmill;
Sheriff Brady and Hindman in Lincoln he slew,
Then he rode to John Chisum's along with his crew.

There he stood off a posse and drove them away,
In McSween's house in Lincoln he made his next play;
Surrounded he fought till the house was burned down,
But he dashed through the flames and escaped from the town.

Young Billy rode north and Young Billy rode south,
He plundered and killed with a smile on his mouth,
But he always came back to Fort Sumner again
For his Mexican sweetheart was living there then.

His trackers were many, they followed him fast,
At *Arroyo Tiván* he was captured at last;
He was taken to Lincoln and put under guard,
And sentenced to hang in the old court-house yard.

J. Bell and Bob Ollinger watched day and night,
And Bob told Young Billy he'd made his last fight.
Young Billy gave Ollinger scarcely a glance,
But sat very still and awaited his chance.

One day he played cards with J. Bell in the room,
Who had no idea how close was his doom;
Billy slipped off a handcuff, hit Bell on the head,
Then he snatched for the pistol and shot him down dead.

Bob Ollinger heard and he ran to the spot
To see what had happened and who had been shot;
Young Billy looked down from a window and fired,
Bob Ollinger sank to the ground and expired.

Then Young Billy escaped on a horse that was near,
As he rode forth from Lincoln he let out a cheer;
Though his foes they were many he feared not a one,
So long as a cartridge remained in his gun.

But his comrades were dead or had fled from the land,
It was up to Young Billy to play a lone hand;
And Sheriff Pat Garrett he searched far and wide,
Never thinking the Kid in Fort Sumner would hide.

But when Garrett heard Billy was hiding in town,
He went to Pete Maxwell's when the sun had gone down;
The door was wide open, the night it was hot,
So Pat Garrett walked in and sat down by Pete's cot.

Young Billy had gone for to cut him some meat,
No hat on his head and no boots on his feet;
When he saw two strange men on the porch in the gloom,
He pulled his gun quick and backed into the room.

Billy said, Who is that? and he spoke Maxwell's name,
Then from Pat Garrett's pistol the answer it came —
The swift, cruel bullet went true to its mark,
And Young Billy fell dead on the floor in the dark.

So Young Billy Bonney he came to his end,
Shot down by Pat Garrett who once was his friend;
Though for coolness and courage both gunmen ranked high,
It was Fate that decided Young Billy should die.

Each year of his life was a notch in his gun,
For in twenty-one years he had slain twenty-one.
His grave is unmarked and by desert sands hid,
And so ends the true story of Billy the Kid.

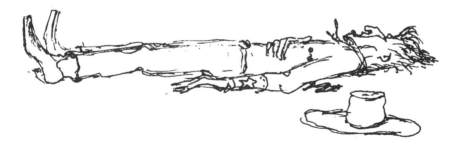

84. *The Raven Visits Rawhide*

Direct confrontations between good and evil, God and Satan, faith and blasphemy, have been verbalized since the year one. In this poem the rivalry between the parson and the saloonkeeper ends in an even draw when the mysterious Raven steps in to quell the fight: a neat way of suggesting that virtue is not at either end but somewhere in the middle. (Hendren 446: manuscript.)

It was meetin' night in Rawhide Town,
And the congregation was settlin' down
To hear the sermon of Parson Brown,
　　When hell broke loose again.
Next door in Hank's Cafe Paree,
The boss was off on his weekly spree,
And settin' 'em up to the cowmen free
　　From a barrel of nigger gin.

The parson strained his lungs to shout,
But Hank's rejoicin' drowned him out,
The devil was winnin' without a doubt
　　And heaven's hopes looked slim.
The parson paused, then shouted, "Men,
The time's at last appointed when
We'll beard the devil in his den,
　　And have it out with him."

Out of the church with his little flock,
The parson paraded down the block,
Lifted the latch without a knock,
　　And entered the hall of sin.
The music ended, the laughter died,
Tongues went speechless and eyes grew wide,
As the parson calmly stepped inside,
　　And the others followed in.

For an instant no one dared to speak,
Even the parson's knees were weak.
He'd forgot the vengeance he'd planned to wreak,
　　And Hank looked on with a frown.
But Hank was not so easily downed,
He grabbed a glass and held his ground
And ordered the boys to drink a round
　　To the parson of Rawhide Town.

"It's the bottoms up!" the barkeeper cried,
"We'll drink to hell where we'll all be fried,
Where we'll cast our souls that are crimson-dyed,
    In the tears our women shed."
The toast was drunk, then Hank stepped up,
Offered the parson a brimmin' cup,
And said, "Drink up, you prayin' pup,
    And trot on home to bed."

Hank laughed when suddenly out on the floor,
A stranger stepped with a forty-four —
And Hank was looking into the bore,
    And wond'ring what to do.
The stranger was lean and hard and small,
And he spoke words with a lazy drawl,
He said, "Now, boys, now listen all,
    And I'll have a word with you.

"I ain't the kind to be buttin' in,
And I'll prob'ly never be here again,
But, boys, I'm mad — I'm mad as sin,
    And I'm going to have my say.
Take my advice and don't get rough.
I'm called the Raven, and boys, I'm tough.
If you think I ain't, jes' call my bluff,
    Now, pray, you buzzards, pray."

Down in the dirt on the rum-soaked floor,
The cowmen knelt till their knees were sore.
And they prayed as they'd never prayed before,
    To save their souls from hell.
And when the parson said amen,
They followed him out of the devil's den,
And they swore they'd be different men,
    But they crossed their fingers well.

The Raven and Hank were left alone,
And the Raven spoke in a gentle tone.
He said, "I'm sorry you pulled that bone,
    For your technique sure is bad!
My sole intentions in comin' here
Was merely to buy a round of beer,
And lift your roll, but now I fear
    I've run things in a ditch.

Continued

"So open your poke and spill the dough,
And I'm beggin' your pardon as I go
That I had to spoil your little show,
    'Cause our ideas didn't hitch."

Hank looked twice at the forty-four
And decided he'd better act before
His guest became a trifle sore,
    So he shoved the roll across the floor.
The Raven bid him a soft good night,
Lifted his gun and blinked the light,
Slammed the door and was off in flight,
    Ridin' the parson's horse.

85. *Silver Jack's Religion*

Though a cowboy or miner wasn't expected to do much about religion, an out-and-out atheist was not tolerated: witness the vigorous way in which Silver Jack converted Robert Waite! (FAC III 125: newspaper clipping ascribing authorship to "John P. Jones, former senator from Nevada.")

I was on the drive in sixty, working under Silver Jack,
Which the same is now in Jackson and ain't soon expected back,
And there was a chap among us by the name of Robert Waite
Who was kinder slick and tonguey — I guess he were a graduate.

Bob could gab on any subject from the Bible down to Hoyle
And his words flowed out so easy just as smooth and slick as oil,
He was what they call a "skeptic" and he loved to sit and weave
High-falutin' words together saying what he didn't believe.

One day as we were waiting for a flood to clear the ground,
We all sat smoking niggerhead and hearing Bob expound;
Hell, he said, was a humbug, and he proved as clear as day
That the Bible was a fable; we allowed it looked that way.

As for miracles and such-like, 'twas more than he could stand,
And for Him they called the Savior, He was just a common man.
"You're a liar!" shouted someone, "and you've got to take
      that back!"
Then everybody started, 'twas the voice of Silver Jack.

Jack clicked his fists together and he shucked his coat and cried,
"'Twas by that th'ar religion my mother lived and died,
And although I haven't always used the Lord exactly right,
When I hear a chump abuse Him he must eat his words or fight."

Now Bob he warn't no coward and he answered bold and free,
"Stack your duds and cut your capers, for you'll find no flies
      on me."
And they fit for forty minutes and the boys would hoot and cheer,
When Jack choked up a tooth or two and Bob he lost an ear.

Continued

At last Jack got Bob under and he slugged him onct or twict,
Then Bob finally admitted the divinity of Christ.
Still Jack kept reasoning with him till the cuss begun to yell,
And allowed he'd been mistaken in his views concerning Hell!

Thus that controversy ended and they riz up from the ground,
And someone found a bottle and kindly passed it round;
And we drank to Jack's Religion in a quiet sort of way,
So the spread of infidelity was checked in camp that day.

86. *Rattlin' Joe's Prayer*

Despite an external show of a whole parcel of traits that seem to flow at crosscurrents with the good old religion, right down inside the punchers were Christian: witness Rattlin' Joe's burial sermon for Monte Bill McCune, using a deck of cards for his text. Captain John Wallace (Jack) Crawford is the author. (Wallace and Frances Rice, *The Humbler Poets: A Collection of Newspaper and Periodical Verse, 1885 to 1910.* Chicago: A. C. McClurg & Co., 1910. Pp. 275–78.)

Jist pile on some more o' them pine knots,
An' squat yoursel's down on this skin,
An', Scotty, let up on yer growlin' —
The boys are all tired o' yer chin.
Alleghany, jist pass round the bottle,
An' give the lads all a square drink,
An' as soon as yer settled I'll tell ye
A yarn as 'll please ye, I think.

'T was the year eighteen hundred an' sixty,
A day in the bright month o' June,
When the Angel o' Death from the Diggin's
Snatched "Monte Bill" — known as M'Cune.
Wal, Bill war a favorite among us,
In spite o' the trade that he had,
Which are gamblin'; but — don't you forget it —
He often made weary hearts glad;
An', pards, while he lay in that coffin,
Which we hewed from the trunk o' a tree,
His face war as calm as an angel's
An' white as an angel's could be.

An' thar's whar the trouble commenced, pards;
Thar war no Gospel sharps in the camps,
An' Joe said, "We can't drop him this way,
Without some directions or stamps."
Then up spoke old Sandy M'Gregor:
"Look'ee yar mates, I'm reg'lar dead stuck,
I can't hold no hand at religion,
An' I'm feared Bill's gone in out o' luck.
If I knowed a darned thing about prayin',
I'd chip in and say him a mass,
But I ain't got no show in the lay-out,
I can't beat the game, so I pass."

Continued

Rattlin' Joe war the next o' the speakers,
An' Joe war a friend o' the dead;
The salt water stood in his peepers,
An' these are the words as he said:
"Mates, you know as I ain't any Christian,
An' I'll gamble the good Lord don't know
That thar lives sich a rooster as I am
But thar once war a time long ago,
When I war a kid, I remember,
My old mother sent me to school,
To the little brown church every Sunday —
Whar they said I war dumb as a mule,
An' I reckon I've nearly forgotten
Purty much all thet ever I knew.
But still, if ye'll drop to my racket,
I'll show ye jist what I kin do.

"Now I'll show *you* my Bible," said Joseph —
"Jist hand me them cards off that rack;
I'll convince ye that this *are* a Bible";
An' he set to work shufflin' the pack.
He spread out the cards on the table,
An' begun kinder pious-like: "Pards,
If ye'll jist cheese yer racket an' listen,
I'll show ye the Pra'ar Book in cards.

"The 'ace' that reminds us of one God,
The 'deuce' of the Father an' Son,
The 'tray' of the Father an' Son, Holy Ghost,
For, ye see, all them three are but one.
The 'four-spot' is Matthew, Luke, Mark, an' John,
The 'five-spot' the Virgins who trimmed
Thar lamps while yet it was light o' the day,
And the five foolish Virgins who sinned.
The 'six-spot' — in six days the Lord made the world,
The sea, an' the stars in the heaven;
He saw it war good w'at He made, then He said,
'I'll jist go the rest' on the 'seven.'
The 'eight-spot' is Noah, his wife an' three sons,
An' Noah's three sons has their wives;
God loved the hull mob, so bid 'em embark —
In the freshet He saved all their lives.
The 'nine' war the lepers of Biblical fame,
A repulsive and hideous squad —
The 'ten' are the holy Commandments, which came

To us perishin' creatures from God.
The 'queen' war of Sheba in old Bible times,
The 'king' represents old king 'Sol.'
She brought in a hundred young folks, gals an' boys,
To the King in his Government hall.
They were all dressed alike, an' she axed the old boy
(She'd put up his wisdom as bosh)
Which war boys an' which gals. Old Sol said, 'By Joe,
How dirty their hands! Make 'em wash!'
And then he showed Sheba the boys only washed
Their hands and a part o' their wrists,
While the gals jist went up to their elbows in suds.
Sheba weakened, an' shook the king's fists.
Now the 'knave,' that's the devil, an', God, ef ye please,
Jist keep his hands off'n poor Bill.
An' now, lads jist drop on yer knees for a while
Till I draw, and perhaps I kin fill;
An' hevin' no Bible, I'll pray on the cards,
Fur I've showed ye they're all on the squar',
An' I think God'll cotton to all that I say,
If I'm only sincere in the pra'ur.

Jist give him a corner, good Lord — not on stocks,
Fur I ain't such a durned fool as that,
To ax ye fur anything worldly fur Bill,
Kāse ye'd put me up then fur a flat.
I'm lost on the rules o' yer game, but I'll ax
Fur a seat fur him back o' the throne,
And I'll bet my whole stock that the boy'll behave
If yer angels jist lets him alone.
Thar's nothin' 'bout him unless he gets riled,
The boys'll all back me in that;
But if any one treads on his corns, then, you bet,
He'll fight at the drop o' the hat.
Jist don't let yer angels run over him, Lord,
Nor shut off all't once on his drink;
Break him in kinder gentle an' mild in the start,
An' he'll give ye no trouble, I think.
An' couldn't ye give him a pack of old cards,
To amuse himself once in a while?
But I warn ye right hyar, not to bet on his game,
Or he'll get right away with yer pile.
An' now, Lord, I hope thet ye've tuck it all in,

Continued

189

An' listened to all that I've said.
I know thet my prayin' is jist a bit thin,
But I've done all I kin fur the dead.
An' if I hain't troubled yer Lordship too much—
So I'll cheese it by axin', again,
Thet ye won't let the 'knave' git his grip on poor Bill.
That's all, Lord—yours truly—Amen."

Thet's "Rattlin' Joe's prayer," old pardners,
An'—what! you all snorin'? Say, Lew,
By thunder! I've talked every rascal to sleep,
So I guess I had best turn in too.

87. Cowboy's Salvation Song

The simple universal lessons of fundamentalist Christianity — faith, repentance, obedience — are cast here in the images of the trail herd: man is to God and the angelic hosts as the dogies are to the trail-herd boss and his crew. The author is Robert Carr. (*Black Hills Ballads.* Denver: Reed Publishing Co., 1902. P. 27.)

Oh, it's move along, you dogies, don't be driftin' by th' way,
Fer there's goin' to be a round-up an' a cuttin'-out they say,
Of all th' devil's dogies an' a movin' at sunrise,
An' you'd better be preparin' fer a long drive to th' skies.

Oh, it's move along, you dogies, don't be driftin' by the way,
Fer th' boss of all th' rus'lers is a-comin' 'round to-day.
So you'd better be a-movin', throw your dust right in his eyes,
An' hit th' trail a-flyin' fer th' home-ranch in th' skies.

So it's move along, you dogies, fer th' devil has in hand
A bunch of red-hot irons an' he's surely goin' to brand
All his dogies, an' some others, an' mighty suddin, too,
So you'd better be a-movin' so he won't be brandin' you.

So it's move along, you dogies, tho' you have th' mange o' sin,
There's a range you're sure to shake it when you come a-trailin' in,
Where th' grass is allers growin' an' th' water's allers pure,
So it's move along, you dogies, 'fore th' devil brands you sure.

88. *Empty Saddles*

For cowboys, as for other Christians, death is an idealized kind of
continuity of life here upon the earth. The empty saddles are, of course,
symbols of range comrades who have died. (PNFQ 142.)

Empty saddles in the old corral,
Where do ya ride tonight?
Are you roundin' up the dogies,
    The strays of long ago?
    Are ya on the trail of buffalo?

Empty saddles in the old corral,
Where do ya ride tonight?
Are there rustlers on the border,
    Or a band of Navajo?
    Are ya heading for the Alamo?

Empty boots covered with dust,
Where do ya ride tonight?
Empty guns, covered with rust,
Where do you talk tonight?

Empty saddles in the old corral,
My tears will be dried tonight
If you'll only say I'm lonely,
    As ya carry my old pal,
    Empty saddles in the old corral.

89. *Star of the Western Skies*

Here the wagon train becomes a symbol of the stream of life itself, and the "West" a symbol of the ultimate goal. The guiding star gives a warm Christian glow. (Hendren 178: manuscript.)

Lonely caravan a-rollin' through the night,
　Lonely caravan, you know the trail is right,
For a guiding star shines from afar,
　Leads the wagon train along.

Stars of the western skies, keep guiding me
　Over hill and dale and winding trail and over the great divide.
Land of the western skies, abide in me,
　For on the darkest night your light shall be my guide.

Wheels a grinding as we're winding on and on
　Through the night and through the coming dawn.
Stars of the western skies, keep on guiding me
　Till my restless heart is satisfied.

90. *The Range Rider's Soliloquy*

What Christians have called "heaven" is usually little more than a selection and sanctification of the best there is in life itself. This cowboy version is typical. (E. A. Brininstool, *Trail Dust of a Maverick*. New York: Dodd, Mead and Company, 1914. Pp. 22–23.)

Sometimes when on night-herd I'm ridin', and the stars are a-gleam
      in the sky,
Like millions of wee, little candles that twinkle and sparkle on high,
I wonder, if up there above 'em, are streets that are shinin'
      with gold,
And if it's as purty a country as all the sky-pilots hev told?

I wonder if there are wide ranges, and rivers and streams that's
      as clear,
And plains that's as blossomed with beauty as them that I ride
      over there?
I wonder if summertime breezes up there are like zephyrs that blow
And croon in a cadence of sweetness and harmony down
      here below?

I wonder if there, Over Yonder, it's true that there's never no night,
But all of the hours are sunny and balmy and pleasant and bright?
I wonder if birds are a-singin' as sweetly through all the long day
As them that I hear on the mesa as I go a-lopin' away?

And sometimes I wonder and wonder if over that lone Great Divide
I'll meet with the boys who have journeyed across to the dim
      Farther Side?
If out on them great starry ranges some day in the future, I, too,
Shall ride on a heavenly bronco when earth's final round-up
      is through?

They tell us no storms nor no blizzards blow over that
      bloom-spangled range;
That always and ever it's summer—a land where there's never
      a change;
And nights when I lie in my blankets, and the star-world casts
      o'er me a spell,
I seem to look through on the glories that lie in that great
      Home Corral.

91. *Desert School Ma'am*

As communities emerged in the West, schools were established and young women from the East were engaged as teachers. Here we have an image of this bleak frontier environment as seen by an idealistic young woman who came to help the frontiersmen regain a hold on their past. Sobina Andrews is the author. (Hendren 166: manuscript.)

All day the sad wind moans and cries
    Around my desert cabin door.
Dust-laden gusts each find a place
    To scatter sand across the floor.

Above the sage the buzzards glide
    Seeking the carcass of last night's calf.
Broken, bereft, the mother cow bawls
    While coyotes slink away and laugh.

At night the pack rat climbs about
    With step as heavy as horse's tread,
The morning finds my carrots gone
    Safely cached beneath the shed.

Yet I must teach this desert school,
    Faithfully three R's I give,
To children small so they forsooth
    May find a better place to live.

92. *A Little Indian Maid*

Many songs and poems praise the Indian as a noble savage, abused
and disinherited by the Anglo-American: catharsis for a very heavy
conscience. Here the Indian's redemption is achieved by the gift of
Christianity made by a still nobler human—the white man, of course.
(Hendren 463: manuscript.)

Through the ancient woods and forest wild
My father roamed while Nature smiled,
With tomahawk and bended bow
To lay the wolf and the red deer low.

My mother in her wigwam sat
To weave the splints of various shade,
To dress the meat, to tan the skin,
And to sew my father's moccasins.

My brothers in their bark canoe
Across the lakes so gaily flew
To shoot the wild ducks in the brakes
Or to catch the whitefish in the lakes.

While a poor little Indian maiden
With acorn shell and wild flowers played
Or by my mother sat all day
To weave and paint the baskets gay.

I could not read nor write nor sew,
My Savior's name I did not know
My parents I oft disobeyed
And to thy Lord I never prayed.

Till white men to the forest came
And taught poor Indians Jesus' name.
They built a church and a schoolhouse near,
With holy hymns the woods did cheer.

Now I can read and write and sew,
My Savior's name I'm taught to know,
My Savior's name I do implore,
God bless the white man evermore.

93. *Gift of the Sego Lily*

Utah's "Dixie" is a bleak strip of desert made fertile by the winding thread of the capricious Virgin River and bound by vertical cliffs of red sandstone. In the 1860s Mormon settlers tilled and irrigated its sparse arable land; for a decade it was touch-and-go as to whether the Saints or raw nature would win. Mabel Jarvis is the author. (FMC III 27.)

So sunbaked, barren, bleak, and full of tears,
The country seemed. So endless stretched the years;
One Pioneer woman, weeping, said that not
One single sign of art, one lovely spot,
One evidence of beauty could she see.
And when her husband begged to disagree,
She bade him bring one gift of loveliness,
One tiny flower to pin upon her dress,
And she would praise his country in her song,
Cease weeping, and be glad the whole day long.

Day after day, as from his toil returning,
With shouldered shovel, he was searching, yearning
For that small floral gift that should bring peace
Into his home, and bitter tears would cease.

At length his patient seeking found reward,
No lovelier diadem can earth afford
Than those sweet Sego Lilies which he brought,
Whose brown eyes in their lavender chalice sought
The face of her who said no art was found
In all these many, many miles around.

She clasped them to her heart and blest the hand
Of him with whom she came to Dixieland.

94. *Ai Viva Tequila*

In the Anglo-Americans' caste system the Mexicans, who preceded them in the Southwest, were just a little above the Indians. Here a Mexican cowboy is chided for drunkenness. (Hendren 53: manuscript.)

Don Pedro is not such a roper,
At ridin' he's none of the best,
But he is the tops as a toper,
Borracho, a star of the west.

And when he is plowing a furrow
He carries a bottle along,
A drink for himself and his burro
And this is his favorite song:

"*Ai viva Tequila,*
It's making me feel-a so fine,
Ai viva Tequila,
Caramba, it's better than wine.

"Without a care-o, I swing my bolero
Right over the Mexican Line.
Ai viva Tequila,
Mucha *tequila* for mine."

95. *Bill and Parson Sim*

This is a full-blown homespun ballad about comradeship, love, violence, murder, and suicide. Buck Berry's daughter, Val, packed such a wallop of feminine charm that the mere question of who should tote her home caused a ballroom brawl that ended in the death of a dozen cowboys! Cleopatra's charm was small, indeed, by comparison! (Hendren 8: manuscript.)

Bill Riley was a cowboy and a quicker shot than him
There wasn't in the country, exceptin' Parson Sim.
And I reckon you could ride the trail from Texas to the line
And braver men than Bill and Sim I'll bet you couldn't find.
Bill, he was tall and lanky with black and piercing eyes
That seemed to flash like lightnin' when storm is in the skies.

His voice was soft and solemn-like, his heart was kind and true,
But he could paint the town as red as any man I knew.
Sim, he was mighty near as tall, with sunny eyes of blue
That seemed to laugh and sparkle, as eyes will sometimes do.
The boys they called him Parson, he owed it to his hair,
And to the classic language he'd use when he would swear.

They chummed as boys together and learned to shoot and ride,
Worked for the same cow out-fits, and grew up side by side.
One bed it always done for both, they used the same war sack,
Stuck up for one another, and all their money'd whack.
Well, Bill and Sim one winter, 'twas back in eighty-nine,
Were batchin' near a tradin' post up north close to the line—

And they was havin' rafts of fun and spendin' lots of coin
Between the little tradin' post and Old Fort Assenboin.
But one night they took in a dance and there they met a gal,
'Twas old Bucky Berry's daughter, his oldest daughter Val.
Her right name was Valentine, they called her Val for short,
She was as fine a little rose as bloomed in that resort.

Her hair was kinder yaller and shined like placer gold,
And on the hearts of Bill and Sim she got an awful hold.
So when she danced with other men, well, Bill he'd hit the rag,
And when Sim couldn't get her smiles he, too, would want a jag.
Waltz, quadrille, and polka was danced till break of day,
And both the fiddlers got so drunk the darn chumps wouldn't play.

Continued

Old Berry he was loaded too and pulled his forty-five,
And worked upon one musician like bees upon their hive.
But ne'er a tune could Berry with all his labor get,
The women folks put on their wraps and dancin' had to quit.
'Twas then the bloody fight was fit, the worst I ever saw,
And I have seen some red hot scraps come off without a flaw.

You see, Bill was stalking 'round, intoxicated quite,
On Love and Injun whiskey, and itchin' for a fight.
While Parson Sim he, too, had on a pretty decent load
And tackled Val to take her home in language *a la mode.*
But just as he was askin' her and she got up to go
Bill he came up to where they was a walkin' kind of slow.

And with a sort of stately bow he turned his back on Sim
And asked Val if she wouldn't take the homeward ride with him.
Well, 'twas over in a second, a few cuss words was said,
Sim he was grazed along the cheek and Bill's was through his head.
And there poor Bill lay bleedin', a-gaspin' hard for breath,
With Sim a-standin' over him, his face as white as death.

A look of horror crossed his face and sorrow filled his eyes
As Bill's brave spirit left the clay and started for the skies.
I reckon that he thought of how in all those happy years
They both had been like brothers and shared their joys and fears.
Then moanin'-like he took the gal and started for the door,
For she had fainted dead away when Bill dropped to the floor.

And with a yell some pulled their guns and made a sudden rush,
They tho't they held a winnin' hand, but Sim he had a flush.
Fer now his fightin' blood was up, and layin' Val aside
To get her out of danger, he let the bullets slide.
Old Buck he got his gal away, then he came back to fight,
But everything was over and he saw an awful sight.

The punchers they was lyin' round, a dozen men or more,
Looked like the field of Gettysburg, so many strewed the floor.
And Parson Sim was dyin' with his arms around poor Bill
His head a-lyin' on the breast that now was cold and still.
He'd won the fight, though wounded, then kneelin' by the spot
Where Bill was lyin' cold in death he fired the fatal shot

That let him follow after Bill, he died without a groan,
And with Bill restin' in his arms he sought the great unknown.
We laid them on a sunny hill, they're sleepin' side by side
Beneath the western prairie soil where once they used to ride.
And Val she never married, and sometimes comes to weep
And wet the flowers with her tears where both her lovers sleep.

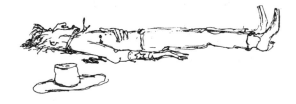

96. *Git Along, Cayuse*

The wanderlust, perennial theme of lyric poetry, is expressed here
with splinter-sharp images from the lives of cowboys who roamed the
cattle country. (Hendren 5: manuscript. We have traced stanzas 1, 2,
and 9 to poems by Henry Herbert Knibbs, but have never been able
to find the poem complete as in the Hendren manuscript.)

Arizona! the tramp of cattle,
   The biting dust and the raw red brand,
Shuffling sheep and the smoke of battle,
   The upturned face and the empty hand.

Dawn and dusk, and the wide world singin'
   Songs that thrilled with the pulse of life,
As we clattered down with our rein chains ringin'
   To woo you — but never to make you wife.

I was top hand once for the T-Bar-T
   In the days of long ago,
But I took to seein' the scenery
   Where the barbed wire fence don't grow.

I was top hand once, with the trail for mine
   And plenty of room to roam,
So now I'm riding the old chuck line
   And any old place is home.

I was top hand once, with the trail for mine,
   Git along, cayuse, git along.
But now I'm feedin' and feelin' fine,
Some folks eat and some folks dine,
   Git along, cayuse, git along.

Seems like I don't get anywhere,
   Git along, cayuse, git along,
But we're leavin' here and goin' there,
   Git along, cayuse, git along.

With little old Josh that steps right free
And my old gray pack-horse, Filaree,
The world ain't got no ropes on me,
   Git along, cayuse, git along.

There ain't no water and there ain't no shade,
There ain't no beer or lemonade —
But I reckon most likely we'll make the grade,
   Git along, cayuse, git along.

One time I had a right good pal,
   Git along, cayuse, git along,
But he quit me cold for a little ranch gal;
   Git along, cayuse, git along.

And now he's took to pitching hay
On a ranch down San Andreas way,
He's done tied up and he's got to stay,
   Git along, cayuse, git along.

97. *Poker*

The poker game is classical among the stereotyped themes of cowboy and western literature. This one, of an untold number of "To be or not to be" parodies, captures the dramatic tension of the game and offers its basic terminology. (Slason Thompson, *The Humbler Poets, 1870–1885*. Chicago: A. C. McClurg & Co., 1899. Pp. 449–50.)

To draw, or not to draw, that is the question.
Whether it is safer in the player to take
The awful risk of skinning for a straight,
Or, standing pat, to raise 'em all the limit.
And thus, by bluffing, get it. To draw—to skin;
No more—and by that skin to get a full,
Or two pairs, or the fattest bouncing kings
That luck is heir to—'tis a consummation
Devoutly to be wished. To draw—to skin;
To skin! perchance to burst—ay, there's the rub!
For in the draw of three what cards may come,
When we have shuffled off the uncertain pack,
Must give us pause. There's the respect
That makes calamity of a bobtail flush;
For who would bear the overwhelming blind,
The reckless straddle, the wait on the edge,
The insolence of pat hands, and the lifts
That patient merit of the bluffer takes,
When he himself might be much better off
By simply passing? Who would trays uphold,
And go out on a small progressive raise,
But that the dread of something after call,
The undiscovered ace-full, to whose strength
Such hands must bow, puzzles the will,
And makes us rather keep the chips we have
Than be curious about the hands we know not of.
Thus bluffing does make cowards of us all,
And thus the native hue of a four-heart flush
Is sicklied with some dark and cussed club,
And speculators in a jack-pot's wealth
With this regard their interest turn away
And lose the right to open.

98. *Bill Roy*

"Bill Roy" implants upon the American frontier a drama of love, elopement, and revenge such as is encountered frequently in English and Scottish ballads. It is, in fact, a parody of "Lady LeRoy." Molly's love for her cowboy is such that she is willing to flout paternal advice and, disguised, to purchase a cavvy from her own father in order to elope with a *gringo* lover. (Gordon 2116.)

The sun was just rising, shone all o'er the plains,
The cavvy was bucking, all nature seemed strange.
I spied a fair couple on old Mexico's shore
A viewing the country all over and o'er.

The one was a Spanish girl, pretty and fair,
The other a *vaquero* persuading his dear,
Persuading his jewel to cross the wild plains,
To the city of Cheyenne, the city of fame.

"Pretty Molly, pretty Molly, the girl I adore,
To leave you behind me would grieve my heart sore.
Your father's an old calender,* and he's angry with me,
To stay in old Mexico my ruin he'd be."

Now this girl being in trouble, she hung down her head,
And then she looked up with more courage and said,
"I've resolved to go with you, we shall have a convoy
And a fine lot of mustangs to give us much joy."

She dressed herself up in *vaquero*'s best clothes
And unto her father in this guise she goes.
She purchased the mustangs, paid down the demand,
Little thought he 'twas done by his own daughter's hand.

Then they saddled their mustangs, their spurs they let roll
As they dashed o'er the prairie, to Cheyenne their goal.

---

*The word perplexes us. Webster gives "a member of an order of wandering dervishes among the Sufis." Or does it refer to a man who operates a calendering machine?

Now when her father came this to understand
He swore his revenge on the contempting young man.
He swore pretty Molly should ne'er be his wife
And for her disobedience he would take her sweet life.

He went to his greasers in a fit of despair
And there he told them the whole affair.
He told them to pursue them, their lives to destroy,
For she ne'er should wed her lover Billy Roy.

Then the greasers made ready, made ready for a fight,
A fight with the cowboys their only delight.
They saddled their mustangs, their whips they threw by
To start on the trail of the daring Bill Roy.

They had not been gone but a week or ten days
And the cowboys were causing the cowtrails to blaze,
When they spied some *vaqueros* and hailed them with joy,
And among them pretty Molly and her lover Bill Roy.

So they bade them come back to old Mexico's shore
Or they from their pistols bright fire would pour.
But the brave young cowboys gave back this reply,
"For the sake of Bill's sweetheart we'll fight 'til we die."

From pistols and pistols the bright fire poured,
And louder than thunder the old rifles roared.
The cowboys gained victory and sweet liberty,
And now I'm a cowboy, both happy and free.

To the city of Cheyenne, the city of fame,
The name of this couple I'll mention again—
The one pretty Molly, her lover Bill Roy,
Sam Wilson, young cowboy, who had the convoy.

99. *Lasca*

The supreme sacrifice, in the name of love, has always been a topic of
ballad and song. "Lasca" is a southwestern example thereof in which
the drama is heightened by the spice of a cross-cultural attachment and
the fearfulness of a cattle stampede. The author is Frank Desprez.
(*Montana Live-Stock Journal*, June 16, 1888.)

I want free life and I want fresh air,
And I sigh for the canter after the cattle,
The crack of a whip's like shots in a battle,
The medley of horns and hoofs and heads
That wars and wrangles and scatters and spreads
And dash and danger and life and love.
And Lasca!
       Lasca used to ride
On a mouse-grey mustang close to my side,
With blue serape and bright belled spur;
I laughed with joy as I looked at her!
Little she knew of books or of creeds:
An Ave Maria sufficed her needs;
Little she cared save to be by my side,
To ride with me, and ever to ride,
From San Saba's shore to Lavaca's tide.
She was as bold as the billows that beat,
She was as wild as the breezes that blow;
From her little head to her little feet
She was swayed in her suppleness to and fro
By each gust of passion; a sapling pine,
That grows on the edge of a Kansas bluff,
And wars with the wind when the weather is rough,
Is like this Lasca, this love of mine.

She would hunger that I might eat,
Would take the bitter and leave me the sweet;
But once, when I made her jealous for fun,
At something I'd whispered or looked or done,
One Sunday, in San Antonio,
To a glorious girl on the Alamo,
She drew from her garter her dear little dagger,
And — sting of a wasp! — it made me stagger!
An inch to the left or an inch to the right,
And I shouldn't be maundering here to-night;

But she sobbed, and, sobbing, so swiftly bound
Her torn *reboso* about the wound,
That I quite forgave her. Scratches don't count
    In Texas, down by the Rio Grande.

Her eye was brown—a deep, deep brown;
Her hair was darker than her eye;
And something in her smile and frown,
Curled crimson lip and instep high,
Showed that there ran in each blue vein,
Mixed with the milder Aztec strain,
The vigorous vintage of old Spain.
She was alive in every limb
With feeling, to the finger tips;
And when the sun is like a fire,
And sky one shining soft sapphire,
One does not drink in little sips.

          *   *   *

The air was heavy, the night was hot,
I sat by her side and forgot—forgot;
Forgot the herd that were taking their rest,
Forgot that the air was close opprest,
That the Texas norther comes sudden and soon
In the dead of night or the blaze of noon;
That once let the herd at its breath take fright,
Nothing on earth can stop the flight;
And woe to the rider, and woe to the steed,
Who falls in front of their mad stampede!

          *   *   *

Was that thunder? I grasped the cord
Of my swift mustang without a word,
I sprang to the saddle and she clung behind.
Away! on a hot chase down the wind!
But never was fox-hunt half so hard,
And never was steed so little spared,
For we rode for our lives, you shall hear how we fared,
    In Texas, down by the Rio Grande.

Continued

The mustang flew, and we urged him on;
There was one chance left, and you have but one;
Halt, jump to ground and shoot your horse;
Crouch under his carcass, and take your chance,
And if the steers in their frantic course
Don't batter you both to pieces at once,
You may thank your star, if not, good-bye
To the quickening kiss and the long drawn sigh
And the open air and the open sky,
    In Texas, down by the Rio Grande.

The cattle gained on us, and, just as I felt
For my old six shooter behind in my belt,
Down came the mustang, and down came we,
Clinging together, and — what was the rest?
A body that spread itself on my breast,
Two arms that shielded my dizzy head,
Two lips that hard to my lips were pressed;
Then came thunder into my ears,
As o'er us surged the sea of steers,
Blows that beat blood into my eyes,
And when I could rise —
Lasca was dead!

              *   *   *

I gouged out a grave a few feet deep,
And there in Earth's arms I laid her to sleep;
And there she is lying, and no one knows;
And the summer shines and the winter snows;
For many a day the flowers have spread,
A pall of petals over her head;
And the little grey hawk hangs aloft in the air,
And the sly coyote trots here and there,
And the black snake glides and glitters and slides
Into a rift in a cottonwood tree;
And the buzzard sails on,
And comes and is gone,
Stately and still like a ship at sea;
And I wonder why I do not care
For the things that are like the things that were,
Does half my heart lie buried there,
    In Texas, down by the Rio Grande?

100. *Young Companions*

Cowboys had bouts with their consciences over the disparity between their actual lives and the precepts instilled in youth by their families, especially their mothers. "Young Companions," an old-world ballad transplanted in the West in multiple forms, is typical. (John R. Craddock, "Songs the Cowboys Sing." *Publications of the Texas Folk-Lore Society,* Vol. VI (1934). Pp. 186–87. Reprinted by permission of the Texas Folklore Society.)

Come all my young companions, wherever you may be
And I'll tell you all a story, to shun bad company.
My home's in Arizona, among those desert hills
My childhood and my fireside are in my memory still.

I had a darling old mother, she always prayed for me,
The very last words she uttered were a prayer to God for me,
Says, "Oh, keep my boy from evil, may God direct his ways,
My blessings are upon you throughout your manhood days."

Well, I bid adieu to loved ones, to kind friends bid farewell,
I landed in Chicago, the very depths of hell.
'Twas there I took to drinking, I sinned both night and day
And ever in my bosom those feeble words would say:

"God keep my boy from evil, may God direct his ways,
My blessings are upon you throughout your manhood days."
While I courted a fair young damsel, her name I will not tell,
For why should I disgrace her since I am doomed for hell?

It was on a moonlit evening, the stars were shining bright
When I drew my ugly dagger and bade her spirit take flight.
The justice overtook me, as well as you now may see
My soul is doomed forever, throughout eternity.

And ever in my bosom those dying words do say,
"God keep my boy from evil throughout his manhood's day."
I am standing on the scaffold, my moments are not long,
You may forget this singer, but don't forget this song.

101. *Ballad of Cactus Nell*

This ballad is charged with melodrama and a lot besides: a classical female type whose pride is in inverse ratio to her honor; her scorn for a stranger who does not submit to her enticements; her calculated provocation of a duel between the stranger and her whilom squire; an ironic grand finale in which womanhood and virtue belatedly restore triumph over masculine honor. (Hendren 546: newspaper clipping.)

Cactus Nell in gaudy gown
Of a dance hall in a border town
Had tried her wiles on a man who seemed
To read her smiles as he stood and dreamed.
He paid no heed to the tell-tale leer
Of the dance hall queen as she lingered near,
But turned and walked to another place
Removed from the taunt of her painted face.

The she-thing paled with a tang of hate
At the slight implied with his measured gait;
Each step kept telling as words might say,
He despised her breed and the tinselled way,
And she raged within as the dance hall clan
Observed the moves of the silent man.
And she made a vow that the man would pay
For the public slight in the dance hall way.

A whispered word and a hurried plan
Was told in the ear of Diamond Dan,
Who hitched the guns in the belt he wore
As he wandered out on the dance hall floor.
He stopped a bit as an idler would,
Quite close to the place where the stranger stood,
And Nell, with the hate of her creed and race,
Stepped close and spat in the stranger's face.

Then silence fell and the place was still,
Like the stage scene set for a sudden kill.
As the stranger stood and calmly viewed
The leering face of the woman lewd.
Then his eyes were turned till they rested on
Her consort near with his six guns drawn;
A grin crept upon his thin, cold lips,
And his hands rested calmly on his holstered hips.

"I reckon," he said, "there has been a day
When a mother loved you in a mother's way,
And I reckon she prayed as her baby grew
That she'd never be a thing like you.
And so for her and the child she bore
I have only pity and nothing more.
But as for you," turning to Diamond Dan,
"I'm calling you, *hombre,* man to man."

The call was quick as a lightning flash,
And the shots rang out in a single crash,
And Diamond Dan slumped down to the floor,
As the stranger walked to the open door.
Then Cactus Nell stared into empty space,
The blood all gone from her throat and face,
And deep in her heart a something stirred
And her pale lips moved, but no one heard.

Well, the fiddles still squeak in the border town,
And the faro wheels spin as the chips flop down,
And the old-timers look in vain for Nell,
One-time queen of the roadhouse hell.
But stories are afloat and the card sharps say,
She lives in Butte in a humble way.
Married? Sure! And they say her man
Is the guy who called the play on Diamond Dan.

102. *Curly Joe*

A cowboy falls desperately in love with a Latin blue blood who scorns him: within the week the hero is thrown and killed by a broncho—an obvious suicide. It's schmaltzy as all get-out, but western folk have read, sung, recited, and loved it through the first half of this century. (FAC II 257: Idaho files, WPA Writers Project, Library of Congress, n.d.)

A mile below Blue Canyon on the lonely Pinon trail,
Near the little town of Sanctos, nestled in a quiet dale,
Is the grave of a young cowboy whose name is now unknown
Save by a few frontiersmen who call the spot their own.

He was as fine a rider as ever forked a steed,
He was brave and kind and generous, never did a dirty deed,
Curly Joe, the name he went by, was enough, none cared to know
If he ever had another, so they called him Curly Joe.

'Bout a mile from the Sanctos village lived an ex-grandee of Spain
And his daughter, bonny Enza, called the White Rose of the Plain.
Curly loved this high-born lassie since that time so long ago
When he found her on the mountains, lost and blinded by the snow.

But coquettish was fair Enza, 'tis a woman's foolish trait
That has blasted many a manhood like the harsh decrees of fate.
When pressed in earnest language, not flowery but sincere,
For an answer to his question she smiled and shed a tear.

When she answered, "Really, Joe boy, quite wearisome you grow.
Your sister, sir, forever, but your wife, no never, Joe."
Not another word was spoken, in a week poor Joe was dead,
Killed by a bucking bronco, or at least that's what they said.

For many a year the tombstone that marked this cowboy's grave
In quaint and curious language this prophetic warning gave:
"Never hope to win the daughter of the boss that owns the brand,
For I tried it and changed ranges to a far and better land."

103. *Lily of the West*

The frontiersman's code placed romantic love for woman at the pin-
nacle of the value system. Though this love be ill-placed, as is the case
here, it condones violence and it remains steadfast despite deceptions
even by the ladylove herself. The ballad has deep roots in Great
Britain and in pre-cowboy times. (*Beadle's Dime Song Books*, No. 5.
New York: Beadle & Co. 1860. P. 48.)

I just came down from Louisville some pleasure for to find
A handsome girl from Michigan so pleasing to my mind,
Her rosy cheeks and rolling eyes like arrows pierced my breast,
They call her Handsome Mary, the Lily of the West.

I courted her for many a day, her love I thought to gain,
Too soon, too soon, she slighted me which caused me grief and pain,
She robbed me of my liberty, deprived me of my rest,
They call her Handsome Mary, the Lily of the West.

One evening as I rambled down by yon shady grove
I met a lord of high degree conversing with my love.
He sang, he sang so merrily while I was sore oppressed,
He sang for Handsome Mary, the Lily of the West.

I rushed upon my rival, a dagger in my hand,
I tore him from my true love and boldly made him stand.
Being mad to desperation, my dagger pierced his breast,
I was betrayed by Mary, the Lily of the West.

Now my trial has come on and sentenced soon I'll be,
They put me in the criminal box and there convicted me.
She so deceived the jury, so modestly did dress,
She far out-shone bright Venus, the Lily of the West.

Since then I've gained my liberty, I roamed the country through,
I'll travel the city over to find my loved one true,
Although she stole my liberty and deprived me of my rest
I love my Mary still, the Lily of the West.

104. *The Broken Wedding Ring*

Bittersweet songs about the separation and reunion of lovers have always been popular. Among frontiersmen this was especially so since separation was inevitable and the prospect of reunion uncertain. Though highbrow literature scorns such naive devices as broken wedding rings, the fortuitous return of the long lost lover, or frontier maids betrothed to European noblemen, in folk poetry these devices enhance the drama. (Hendren 340: manuscript.)

A cowboy with his sweetheart stood beneath a starlit sky,
Tomorrow he was leaving for the lonesome prairie wide.

She said, "I'll be your loving bride when you return some day."
He handed her a broken ring and to her he did say:

"You'll find upon that ring, sweetheart, my name engraved in gold,
And I will keep the other half, which has your name you know."

He went away to ride and toil, this cowboy brave and bold,
But long he stayed and while he strayed the maiden's love
      grew cold.

Three years had passed, he did not come, and Nell will wed tonight,
Her father said an earl would make her happy home so bright.

The lights were gaily glowing as they stood there side by side,
"Let's drink a toast to this young man and to his lovely bride."

Just then there stood within the door a figure tall and slim,
A handsome cowboy was their guest and slowly he walked in.

"I'll drink with you a toast," said he, and quickly in her glass
He dropped his half of wedding ring, then anxiously he watched.

She tipped her glass and from her lips a ring fell shining bright,
The token she had longed to see lay there beneath the light.

"Tho' years have been between us, dear, love has won our last
      long fight,
It's you, my cowboy sweetheart, and my Jack I'll wed tonight."

216

105. *Prairie Lullabye*

Cowboy and western images are planted even in the minds of infants. Scores of lullabies might be offered as evidence. The images may be prosaic and the metaphors mixed, but babies are not as demanding as grownups. (Hendren 236: manuscript.)

Shadows slowly creeping
  Down the prairie trail,
Everything is sleeping,
  All but the nightingale.
Moon will soon be climbing
  In the purple sky,
Night winds are a humming
  This tender lullabye.

Cares of the day have fled,
  My little sleepy head,
The stars are in the sky,
  Time that your prayers were said,
My little sleepy head,
  To a prairie lullabye.

Saddle up your pony,
  The sandman's here
To guide you down
  The trail of dreams.
Tumble in bed, my baby,
  My little sleepy head,
To a prairie lullabye.

106. *My Little Buckaroo*

(PNFQ 298.)

Close your sleepy eyes,
　My little buckaroo,
While the light of western skies
　Is shining down on you.
Don't you know it's time for bed?
　Another day is through.
So go to sleep,
　My little buckaroo.

Don't you realize,
　My little buckaroo,
It was from a little acorn
　That the oak tree grew?
And remember that your dad
　Was once a kid like you,
So go to sleep,
　My little buckaroo, hmm, humm.

Soon you're gonna ride the range
　Like grown-up cowboys do,
Now it's time that you
　Were roundin' up a dream or two.
So go to sleep,
　My little buckaroo.

107. *Buckaroo Sandman*

(Hendren 168: manuscript.)

It's the Buckaroo Sandman
On his lullaby pony,
Riding over the stardust trail
To rock-a-bye land.

All the Buckaroo cowhands
Bronco pillows are ridin',
Poundin' leather to Sleepy-town
Over Dream Land sand.

At the Baby Land rodeo, to and fro,
Swingin' in the saddle of Dad's elbow.
Giddy-up, giddy-up,
Get a dogie in your dream lasso.

When the daylight is breakin'
Over valley and plain,
In your little corral
Asleep with mother again.

108. *Indian Cradle Song*

Among lullabies Indian images compete with cowboys for first honors — not the hot-blooded Indians of violence and stealth, naturally, but the idealized noble savages of the white man's fantasy. (JL 307: typescript copied from *Dallas Democrat,* Dallas, Texas, May 23, 1914.)

Swing thee low in thy cradle soft
  Deep in the dusky woods,
Swing thee low and swing aloft,
  Swing as a papoose should.
For safe in your little birchen nest
Quiet will come and peace and rest
  If the little papoose is good.

The coyote howls on the prairie wild
  And the owl, it hoots in the tree,
And the big moon shines on the little child
  As it slumbers peacefully.
So swing thee high in thy little nest
And swing thee low and take thy rest
  That the night wind brings to thee.

The father lies on the fragrant ground
  Dreaming of hunt and fight
And the pine leaves rustle with mournful sound
  All through the solemn night.
But the little papoose in his birchen nest
Is swinging low as he takes his rest
  Till the sun brings the morning light.

109. *Denver Dan*

A frail underdog steps into the Silver Star Saloon, drops Denver Dan
and five of his gang, then falls dead, torn shirt exposing her true gender.
Disguised as a gunman, for a year she had stalked the killers of her
lover until at last she found them and wrought her deadly revenge.
(JL 478: manuscript from R. R. "Slim" Critchlow. n.d.)

Denver Dan and his hardboiled gang, atoms of tool and doom,
Larkey and Wright, they stood one night in the Silver Star Saloon,
When the door swung back and a kid in black came strolling
     softly in,
At the bandits glared with a hostile air, and looking mighty grim.

About five foot three he looked to me, and kinda slender too,
And two big gats like baseball bats hung at his hips in view.
At last he spoke, and I hope to choke if it didn't chill me through,
His voice was froze as cold as the snows as he faced that
     lawless crew.

"I've been riding sign on the border line of Canada through
     the states
On the trail of a band that I would follow through hell's own gates.
A year ago up in Idaho they shot my pal Jim Kelly
Who was going away the following day to marry his
     sweetheart Nelly."

"I took the trail through storm and gale, I've been following it
     now for a year,
I followed it close from coast to coast and I'm hoping that
     trail ends here.
Now the man I'm hunting and the man I want more than anyone
     else in the gang,
And I'll shoot the dog as dead as a log, who is known as
     Denver Dan."

Now as smooth as glass and as bold as brass was Denver
     Dan McGrew
But he fought his last fight and he died that night in the
     Silver Star Saloon.
For the kid in black sure had the knack, to the draw his guns
     had wings,
And to us that saw that lightning draw, they seemed like
     living things.

Continued

They seemed to leap to meet the sweep of his hands as they
  flashed in view,
And the cylinders spun as they roared as one, and Denver Dan
  was through.
Then he turned to another who dove for cover too late to
  escape the lead,
And he got four more as he hit the floor with a bullet in his heart,
  stone dead.

And as he slipped his shirt was ripped on the end of the bar
  as he fell,
And there half-exposed was a breast disclosed, 'twas Kelly's
  sweetheart Nell.

110. *Young Jack Snyder*

The Pony Express has had a special place in western lore. Here we are offered the gripping image of a Pony Express rider carrying his precious charge through an ambush of savage Indians, and finally dying violently in line of duty. Jack turns out to be a teen-aged girl. James Barton Adams is said to be the author. (FAC II 101: New Mexico files, WPA Writers Project, Library of Congress, 1936–37.)

It in memory lingers, that boyish form,
    In the corduroys and the soiled *sombrero,*
That dashed from the station in sun or storm,
    On the pony trail an intrepid hero.
We can see the flash of the youthful eyes
    That told of a nature to fear a stranger,
As into the saddle he'd lightly rise,
    With a laugh at the caution, "Look out for danger,"
As he'd snatch the bag from the agent's hand
And dash away on the overland.

He would never join with his pards
    In the wild carouse in the pony stables,
He would never shuffle the greasy cards
    Nor risk a sou at the faro tables.
Profanity never passed his lips,
    Yet he held respect of the rougher faction,
For the guns he wore on his rounded hips
    Were ever ready and quick of action,
And every man at the station knew
The bold boy rider could use them too.

From O'Fallon's Bluffs to the Niggerheads
    On the pony trail there was not a rider
Could hold his own with pursuing Reds
    And give them the slip like young Jack Snyder.
He'd an arrow scar on his boyish cheek
    From the hand of a hidden Red freebooter
Whose hide in a jiffy sprung a leak
    As it caught a ball from the boy's six-shooter,
And he left the Red for ki-o-tee feed,
As he onward sped on his wiry steed.

Continued

But the Injuns got him at last, and when
    The corpse was brought to O'Fallon's station
The wife of the agent told the men
    'Twas a case for a woman's consideration.
We never learned who the brave girl was
    Who'd chosen the work of a Western ranger,
And tried to think 'twas no wicked cause
    That had driven her into a life of danger.
We thought of her only as true and brave
As we laid her away in an unknown grave.

111. *Belle Starr*

Belle Starr is the best known of the women outlaws. Several ballads deal with her and most of them paint a heroic image. The following piece, though roughhewn, contains poetic images and phrases which stick in the mind like thorns: "a sheath of knitted brows," "eyes like watch dogs kenneled in the brain," "we knew her when her fingers strayed on ivory keys." (Hendren 200: manuscript.)

A cowboy hat, and underneath
Two weapons flashing from a sheath
Of knitted brows, brows that are clear
Of storm or wrath. Perhaps once a year
A woman, she, and with such eyes
Like watch dogs kenneled in her brain,
  Woe to the fool who gropes,
Likewise to him who views her with disdain.

A queen self-crowned by self-reliance,
The laws, she holds them in defiance,
Laughs long and loud at sheriff's writ,
And somehow that's the last of it.
But who is she? So indiscreet
Who over-rides you on the street
  Not caring whoever you are
  That's Belle Starr.

Brunette with raven hair is she,
And calls herself a Cherokee,
But who would dare dispute her claim
Or even question whence she came?
  The timid press reporter
Sneaks closer and closer to her gown;
  She turns abruptly, seldom speaks,
But always checks him with a frown
Which plainly means, "Down, Pompey, down!"

Continued

Arrest her! Oh, you try that game?
  In Dallas many years ago
The county sheriff tried the same.
  One rapid shot, the rest you know;
Still Belle loves to give her name:
    "Please let me have your best cigar,
    I'm Belle Starr."

We knew her when her fingers strayed on ivory keys,
  How well she played in Texas, nights long ago,
  But things have changed since then, you know,
  Once when we sought her out one day,
  She laughed full fifty miles away,
  At Dallas fashions and the fools
  Who followed after social rules.

To see her mounted, and with speed
  Ride far into the setting sun,
Meant simply this, a daring deed
  Scarce thought of e'er the deed was done,
With lawless men the most at ease,
She bets and gambles, but you'll please
  Observe she never goes too far—
  That's Belle Starr.

Who says she never loved? He lies!
A woman's heart in such disguise
Must surely be the wreck that hides
When love drifts outwards with the tides.
Alas for those who lived to feel,
The months and years around them reel,
And crumble into space with still
The same old yearning to fulfill.

Be merciful—condemn her not—
By scornful words or evil thoughts,
For should you strike her mountain glen
Where only hide the roughest men,
And tap the door some stormy night,
A voice might bid you to alight—
    "Come in, I care not who you are,
    I'm Belle Starr."

112a. *Queen of the Desperadoes*

We offer another realistic ballad about Belle Starr in two significantly different texts so that readers may appreciate what can happen to a piece of poetry that floats in oral tradition. Both texts bristle with primitive images and speech, suggesting that art at its best is artless. (Hendren 533: newspaper clipping.)

> She was a two-gun woman,
>   Miss Belle Shirley was her name;
> The Lone Star state of Texas
>   Was where she won her fame.
>
> Oh, I was a puncher in an old slouch hat,
> But I couldn't make any money at that,
> So I said to Belle, "Let me join your show,
> If it gets too hot I'll ride to Old Mexico."
>
> Jim Reed was her first lover,
>   And she eloped with him one night,
> While her dad chased them across Texas
>   Trying to stage a fight.
>
> When Jim Reed was drilled by Morris
>   Belle she took to the trail,
> And started a life of wanderin'
>   That everyone knew would fail.
>
> When Belle she married Mr. Starr
>   She moved to Younger's Bend
> And lived on Canadian river
>   Until the very end.
>
> Belle fell from under her steed one day,
>   Traitor Watson was the cause;
> But both of them were guilty—like the rest of us—
>   Of breaking the territory's laws.
>
> Oh, come, cowhands and herders,
>   Every gambler, prospector and bum;
> Don't tinker with gun-totin' ladies
>   Or drink too much nigger-head rum.

Continued

For Belle was a beautiful tough one,
    And she led all her gang to the grave;
But while they were up and kickin'
    Each one of them was her slave.

112b. *Queen of the Desperadoes*

(FAC II 133: from "Songs o' th' Cowboys" corralled by Chuck Haas.)

She was a two-gun woman,
  Belle Shirley was her name.
'Twas in the State of Texas
  Belle won undying fame.

Jim Reed was her first lover,
  Belle eloped one night with him.
Her pap choused 'em crost Texas
  To stage a fight with Jim.

The lovers lived all happy
  Till Jim got in a tight,
And drilled plum through by Morris
  And cashed-in the same night!

When Jim from her was tooken,
  Belle took the wildsome trail,
And starts a life of ramblin'
  Thet shore was bound to fail.

I was a pore young cowboy,
  But money was too slow,
So I joined Belle's wild riders
  In north New Mexico.

We raided the Pan-handle,
  Then holed-up in the Strip.
When we run'd out of money
  We'd make a-nuther trip!

We know'd no Law ner order,
  'Cept purty Belle's command,
As we rid free and reckless
  Acrost that wildsome land.

Then Belle fell sorely wounded.
  'Twas traitor Watson's cause!
Though, like us, he was guilty
  Of breakin' Texas' laws.

Continued

But Belle was soon recovered,
　And I rid by her side. . . .
The last of all her riders!
　By my hand Watson died!

Then Henry Starr Belle married
　And moved to Younger's Bend
On the Canadian River . . .
　She lived thar till the end!

113. *The Ballad of Pug-Nosed Lil*

Here we have the *genre burlesque* at its very best. The stereotypes, clichés, classical images, and dramatic events of frontier life are assembled and ordered with amazing skill, thus producing a rare comic effect. Complex poetic structures reinforce the exuberant good humor of the poem. The author is Robert H. Fletcher. (*Corral Dust: Western Verse.* Helena, Montana, 1936. Pp. 70-73.)

In Rattlesnake Gulch of the Skihootch Range
 Dwelt a miner, Cockeyed Bill,
And his little gal was his only pal,
 She was knowed as Pug-Nosed Lil.
In a cabin neat he had sought retreat
 Where he sheltered her from ills,
While he strove and toiled and delved and moiled
 For the gold in them thar hills.

She may not have been so long on looks
 And her chest was a trifle flat,
But she never played faro and she shunned mascara
 And rouge and the likes of that,
While Bill was a man with a rough hewed pan
 Who at times could be plumb tough.
You can bet this cinch that in any pinch
 They were diamonds in the rough.

On Alkali Creek just across the ridge
 Where the meadowlarks sing sweet,
Lived a young cowpoke with a heart of oak
 Who was knowed as Roundup Pete.
With a passion pure he could scarce endure
 His heart beat 'neath his vest,
For he loved Lil true as the he-men do
 In the great wide open West.

Up Spotted Calf Trail over Freeze-out Flat
 He would ride on his paint cayuse
When his work was through just to court and woo
 By the side of a placer sluice.
Well, he stood ace high and was getting by
 With Bill and the pug-nosed wren
For they both opined he'd a good pure mind, —
 One of nature's noblemen.

Continued

Now a snake in the grass lived at Hell Gate Pass,—
 His soul was as black as tar.
It had been his aim to jump Bill's claim
 On the El Dorado Bar.
He had planned, the skunk, that when Bill got drunk,
 As sometimes a miner does,
He would steal the skirt and would do her dirt
 Like the villainous fiend he wuz.

Old Bill got canned, as the slicker planned,
 Down at Shorty's Sample Bar
Where a lot of ginks let him buy them drinks
 Or a good five cent cigar.
And the villain sneered and he kind of leered
 In a most offensive style
Till he made a crack and Bill came back,
 "When you say that, stranger, smile!"

With Bill in his cups, why, the varmint ups
 And heads out to grab Bill's kid.
He was on the prowl for to do as foul
 A deed as ever was did!
Well, he found the frail waiting by the trail
 That goes to Chimney Butte.
She was lorn and sad for her cockeyed Dad
 For she loved the old galoot.

Cantankerous Nash with the dyed mustache,
 For that was the rascal's name,
Advanced on the maid who was pale and afraid
 And aware now of his game.
To this ornery guy with the shifty eye
 She uttered her favorite line,
"You low down slicker, your breath smells of likker,
 And your lips shall NOT touch mine!"

Now men were men in those old days when
    This circumstance occurred,
And Pete, of course, on his wonder horse
    Had left the thundering herd
For old Bill's shack just to get a snack
    Of the grub like Lil could cook,
When his eye so keen lit upon the scene
    Where Lil fought off the crook.

Down the mountain trail Pete rolled his tail
    To rescue the fair young wren
While the villain cursed till he almost burst
    For the skunk was foiled again.
Pete loudly cried as he reached her side,
    "Leave her be, you dastard rat!"
This Pete was a gent and what he meant
    Was a different word than that.

Nash loosed all holts and he pulled his Colts
    To plug Pete on the spot,
But like a flash Pete socked this Nash
    With a right cross that was hot.
They went to a clinch that was no soft cinch,
    It was root-hog, win, or bust,
And the canyon rang with a bang! bang!! bang!!!
    And the scoundrel bit the dust.

Then Pete took Lil and they found old Bill
    And they looked up a nice J. P.
Who made the splice for a reasonable price,
    Now they're happy as can be.
And in Rattlesnake Gulch of the Skihootch Range
    There is peace and ca'm once more
While the pale moon shineth and the woodbine twineth
    Round the old log cabin door.

Lexicon

(We refer to *Adams* in this section of our study. Full bibliographical reference is: Ramon F. Adams, *Western Words: A Dictionary of the Range, Cow Camp and Trail.* Norman: University of Oklahoma Press, 1946.)

alkali. Basins which accumulate alkaline wastes due to the nature of soils and poor drainage abound in the Great Basin and other regions of the Southwest. The Great Salt Lake and vast saline expanses on its western side are the most notorious examples of this terrain feature. Water in the stream beds is sparse and brakish, and winds hurl salten sands that bite the skin.

Arkansas fence. *See* FENCES.

arroyo. Spanish for *small stream.* In the Southwest it means a precipitous gully or channel cut in soft earth by the waters from sudden violent storms.

bacon's curled. i.e., cooked. Curled bacon as an image of death persists in cowboy and western song and verse.

Badgers. Nickname for inhabitants of Wisconsin.

badlands. Used to identify areas in the West where erosion has been so violent that little or no vegetation remains in a region of buttes, mesas, and other exotic and forbidding forms, and where man and beast find it hard to make their way.

bar. In mining country, the deposits of sand, gravel, or silt which have been laid down along the stream beds by flood waters. Also, in a saloon, the counter at which drinks are served to standing customers.

barbed wire. *See* FENCES.

batching (batch, *v.*). Housekeeping performed by men of the range without female help.

bed ground (bedground), bedded, bedding (cattle). On the range or on trail drives the bed ground was the place where cattle gathered to spend the night. On drives range cattle were skittish: getting them "bedded" took some riding, and guards rode circle on them all night long.

bender, *n.* Cowboys' drunken spree during which they "painted the town red."

bison. *See* BUFFALO.

bit, *n.* Metal bar that traverses a horse's mouth. There are many types, ranging from a straight metal bar to variously curbed or articulated types. Silver mountings and gaudy designs were, like boots, spurs, and sombrero, symbols of affluence or the quest for status.

black snake. Common name for *coluber constrictor,* large, agile North American snake. Also a braided rawhide whip used by bullwhackers, stage drivers, and wagoners.

blind (railroad). Above the coupling which joins two railroad freight cars there is a "blind space" about four feet wide. A bum could stand on the coupling and hang on to steel rungs above him designed to permit railroad employees to climb to the roofs of the cars.

blinds (horse). Shields used on harness horses to cut off side vision. When breaking a horse to saddle, or when riding bucking broncos at a rodeo, vision is cut off completely until the "buckaroo" is seated; then the blind is removed and the animal "takes off."

bolero. Spanish; short open vest, with or without sleeves, worn by both sexes.

boot hill. A name given the frontier cemetery, because most of its early occupants died with their boots on. The word has had an appeal as part of the romantic side of the West and has become familiar as a picture of the violent end of a reckless life. But, to the westerner, boot hill was just a graveyard where there "wasn't nobody there to let 'em down easy with their hats off." Like the old saying, "There ain't many tears shed at a boot-hill buryin'," and it is "full o' fellers that pulled their triggers before aimin'." (Adams, pp. 15–16.)

borracho, *n.* or *adj.* Spanish for *drunk.*

bowie (after Colonel James Bowie [d. 1836], its inventor). A single-edged hunting knife about fifteen inches long; carried by frontiersmen in a leather case hung from the belt.

brand, *n.* Mark burned into the hides of cattle or other animals to identify ownership; *v.*, to put such a mark on an animal. To assure that brands for each owner were distinctive, registration by a state official came into being, and brand books were, and still are, issued periodically. Brands were inflicted with a branding iron, running iron, or simply an iron. On the open range, irons were heated in a small fire. Critters were roped, thrown, and tied, then branded and released. "Reading" or "calling" brands was a necessity whenever cattle of different owners were to be separated. When cattle were sold, old brands were canceled (also with an iron), and the new brand burned on. The expert rustling of branded cattle necessitated careful modification of brands using appropriate irons. Often the brand also became the recognized name for the home ranch; the rancher, and often his ranch hands, might even be known by the brand in lieu of their family names. For specific brands in this study consult the index. In a figurative sense to "start a brand" meant to get married and rear a family. In a transcendental sense brands (of God or Satan) were worn by Christians in a state of grace or disgrace.

break (or bust), unbroke (man), broke. The process of training a horse to ride. Westerners typically didn't have the time or temperament to nurse a horse along; it lived free and wild until needed in the string of saddle horses, when it was lassoed, saddled, and ridden for the first time—an event well remembered by the bronc and also by its buster, if the bronc had any spark, that is. Thereafter the bronc was worked just as if it had some sense until, in effect, it did.

bronc. *See* HORSE.

broomtail. *See* HORSE.

buck, *v.* The efforts of an ungentled horse or wild steer to unseat its rider. Prior to being "broken" almost any range horse will make a most vigorous struggle to "throw" its rider. Adams (p. 22) lists a half-column of names to identify the pitches and other movements that characterize bucking, this terminology being developed as systematically and as comprehensively as is the "lingo" of boxing or wrestling.

buckaroo, *n.* Probably derived from Spanish *vaquero*, influenced by the verb *buck*. It is another name for the cowboy, but generally designates one who is a bit on the rough and cantankerous side. Note its use as an endearing epithet in the lullabies.

buffalo (bison). Name westerners used most commonly to identify *Bison americanus,* majestic and mighty monarch of the plains whose image, especially when on chase or stampede, struck frontiersmen's minds with awe and wonder.

buffalo grass. *Buchloë dactyloides.* Great Plains species of grass well adapted to arid steppe conditions; the principal food of bison and other plains ruminants prior to cultivated exploitation of these areas. It grew to as much as five feet in height.

bug juice. Slang for whiskey.

bulldog (dog). Rodeo sport in which a horseman rides alongside a critter, drops on its neck and throws the animal off its feet. Adams (p. 23) says a Negro puncher, Tom Pickett, was the first to practice the art, and that it appeared first in rodeos as an exhibition only. Now it is a regular part of the rodeo repertoire.

bullwhacker. A man who drove the ox teams in early freighting days. (Adams, p. 24.)

bunch, *n.* A group of cattle; *v.,* to drive a herd of cattle together. (Adams, p. 24.)

buster, *n.* A "hand" who "busts" horses; *v., see* BREAK.

butte. French; a high detached hill or ridge rising steeply from a plain, especially in the Rocky Mountains and vicinity; a small mesa.

buzzard. Otherwise called a *turkey vulture. Cathartes aura,* a large hawk-like scavenger whose range extends from the plains to the Pacific, and from Canada south into Central and South America. Applied to men, it is an epithet of derision.

calaboose. From Spanish *calaboso,* a prison.

call the play, *v.* In a pistol duel, the gunman provoking his adversary to draw.

cañon (canyon). From the Spanish *cañon,* cannon, tube, pipe. In the Southwest it came to mean a gorge.

caramba. Spanish interjection expressing surprise, wonder, or interest.

cardsharp, *n.* Professional gambler, especially one who is expert at cheating.

carne. Spanish for *meat.*

cash in, *v.* To die.

catclaw. Species of *acacia greggii.* Widely spread in the arid regions of the West and Southwest.

catenas. Spanish *cadena,* chain. Probably designates chains about six inches long connecting the bit to the reins. Highly ornamental, they may also have served a practical purpose in preventing rapid deterioration of the ends of the leather reins which otherwise would be continually moistened with saliva from the horse's mouth.

cavvy (also cavyard, cavvy yard, covy-yard). From the Spanish *caballada.* The "string" of horses kept on hand to work cattle on roundup or on trail drive. Syn. *remuda.*

cayuse. *See* HORSE.

chapparal. Term applied to *Atriplex, adanostroma arctostaphilos,* and other genera of thorny evergreen shrubs of the Southwest. Usually more than stirrup high, they form thickets and areas of cover ideal for the protection of range cattle, much to the annoyance of punchers who have to ride through it.

chaps. Spanish, *chaparejos* or *chapareras.* Leather trousers or overalls worn over the ordinary trousers to protect the horseman's legs from injuries caused by brush, fences, etc. Syn. *leggings.*

chili. Sauce made from ground pods of the red (chili) pepper. By extension, a soup using beans, red pepper, and other ingredients.

chin, *v.* Deeds without words are admired by the cowboy; he doesn't like to be "chinned," i.e., talked to.

cholla (chola, choya). *Opuntia fulgida mammillata.* One of the small, tree-like cacti of the arid regions of the Southwest. Nearly spineless, it was found edible by cattle, sheep, and rodents. Curio shops sell lamps, flower holders, and other objects made from its dried shell. It grows to five feet in height.

chuck. Range name for food.

"Chuck away!" Call used by a cowcamp cook to assemble the hands for a meal.

chuckwagon. A wagon equipped to serve as a mobile kitchen for cowboys on trail or roundup.

chute. A narrow, fenced lane, usually connecting one corral with another; also a narrow passage designed for loading cattle into railroad cars, or passing them through into dipping vats. At a rodeo it terminates in a cage just big enough to permit the buckaroo to adjust his gear and mount. When rider is ready, the gate is sprung and the animal goes into action.

cinch, cinching strap. From the Spanish *cincha,* girth or cinch. Girth that passes around the horse's body to anchor the saddle. For heavy work there are generally two.

circle, *n., v.* On roundup a crew of punchers fans out to gather all the cattle on a certain range. The circle riders are those who take the outer perimeter; a circle horse is one chosen with sufficient stamina ("bottom," in cowboy lingo) to endure the greater mileage. On trail drive cattle moved on a broad front to permit grazing as they moved: at night the punchers rode circle to bring them together on the bedding ground. Guards rode circle around them all night long. The image is carried over to analogous figures in a square dance. *See* RIM-MING.

clown (rodeo). At a rodeo the clowns fill empty moments with homely and often vulgar

jokes, usually exchanged with the master of ceremonies. But their unannounced and vital function is to protect the thrown riders from the mad fury of the steers or mustangs by distracting the critters long enough for the buckaroo to get to his feet and clear the nearest fence.

Colt. In 1875 Colt produced a single action 45-calibre pistol known as the Peacemaker. Three years later it appeared in a model accommodating the same 44–40 cartridge used in the Winchester rifle, thus permitting a westerner to carry a single type of cartridge for both rifle and pistol. This new weapon acquired further utility in the West because its sturdy frame recommended it for the gruesome sport of pistol-whipping, an occasional practice whereby marshals clubbed tough hombres over the head, or outlaws intimidated their victims. (Summarized from Larry Koller, *The Fireside Book of Guns.* New York: Simon and Schuster, 1959. Pp. 131–32.)

"Come and git it!" Camp cook's call to chuck.

conchas. Spanish for shell or case. In western lingo, slightly convex metal disks, usually made of silver, used as ornaments on horses' or cowboys' gear.

Concord chains. We have not found any other specific reference to Concord chains. However, Concord was a leading manufacturer of carriages and horse gear of all kinds. A 1906 distributor's catalog shows several pages of harnesses for carriage horses; in almost all of these the ends of the traces consisted of a dozen or more links of chain. When these were attached to the singletree, using any except the last link, it meant that the excess links hung loose and produced an audible jingle when the rig was in motion.

corn juice. One of a score of western synonyms for whiskey.

corral. Enclosure designed to hold cattle, sheep, or horses in a restricted area, usually made of pole fences from five to eight feet high. The "home corral" is the final abode of the human spirit.

cottonwood. Common name for several species of *populus*, the females of which produce seeds carried by tiny flakes of cotton. Widely disseminated in the arid Southwest, especially along stream beds.

cowhand, cowman, cowpoke, cowpuncher. All these terms apply broadly to men who work cattle as their principal occupation. *Cowman* tends to be reserved for an owner or manager; the other for the brawn and muscle men. *Poke, hand,* and *puncher* often stand sans prefix, but with the same meaning. (The work these men perform is known as cowpunching or punching cows.)

coyote. From the Mexican *coyotl. Canis latrans* is of the same genus as the dog and the wolf. His range extended from the Mississippi to the Pacific Coast and from down in Old Mexico to Arctic regions. He has survived the inroads of civilized man: specimens have recently been seen in Los Angeles. His image is encountered more often in western verse than that of any other animal. Natives of South Dakota are called coyotes. To be left for coyote feed was a fate met by many an unredeemed badman, i.e., to be killed and left unburied on the prairies.

crack-a-lou. Gambling game consisting of pitching coins toward the ceiling in a room so that they would fall as near as possible to a crack in the floor.

crick. Typical western word for creek, a stream smaller than a river but somewhat larger than a brook.

critter. Cattle; by extension, other domestic or wild animals, including women.

curreta. Probably Spanish *carreta,* a long, narrow cart.

cut, *n., v.* At a roundup, the range cattle were assembled into smaller units for any number of purposes. It took an expert hand and a well-trained cutting horse to ride into the herd, locate, and isolate the animals as desired. A cut was used to identify an animal or herd, separated from the main group for whatever purpose. The image, transferred to man, meant the selection of souls at the Final Judgment.

dally, *n., v.* In Mexican, ¡*dale vueltas!* or "give it some twists." Anglicized to *dally welters,* then simply *dally.* In roping cattle a full turn is taken around the horn of the saddle at the moment of making a catch. This is done in such a way that the rope can be released at once, or slack can be taken up. If the lasso is tied fast, saddle and rider may be torn from the horse.

desert rat (pack rat, wood rat). *Neotoma lepida* is widely dis-
tributed in the West. In its southernmost range, it gathers cactus stems to build a shelter as a covering over its underground burrow. Legend has not greatly exaggerated its compulsive collectomaniacal habits, though we are less certain about the widely accepted belief that it always leaves something to replace the object of its theft.

diamond back. *See* RATTLE-SNAKE.

dip, *v., n.* To treat cattle for several different maladies they are forced through a narrow chute and into a tank filled with an antiseptic liquid.

dog, *v. See* BULLDOG.

dogie. Scrubby calf, orphan calf, unbranded calf, or calves generally. Derivation is uncertain: Spanish, *dogal,* is a slip or hangman's knot— i.e., a calf fit to be killed? English, *dough-gut,* a lean pot-bellied calf carrying the scars of malnutrition? Human dogies are wrangled to the final roundup where they are cut and driven along the trail to the Home Ranch or to hell.

dough. Slang for money.

drags, *n.* To permit a horse to graze without wandering too far, Westerners sometimes attached a drag, i.e., a heavy weight (log, stone, etc.) to one of the horse's feet.

draw, *n.* Form of poker in which the players, having been dealt five cards, may discard any or all of the cards originally received and have them replaced by an equal number from the deck.

drive, *n.* The organized movement of cattle, on the range or the trail.

dude. Applied by genuine range folk to the city-bred man out in the wide-open spaces merely for kicks.

dungre grass. Neither biologist colleagues nor Webster has been able to inform us about this plant. Is it derivative of *dungaree,* defined by Webster as "a coarse cotton cloth used for tents, sails, work clothing, etc."?

earmark, *n., v.* Earmarks as well as brands are used to indicate ownership; both were frequently inflicted upon the animal at the same time. At roundup the brand caller shouted the name of earmark and brand.

faro. A gambling game with cards, in which the players bet on the cards to be turned up from the top of the dealer's pack. In one of our texts a faro wheel is mentioned. Perhaps this refers to the use of a faro box which prevented delivery of more than one card at a time.

fences. Since fences permit the selective and specialized use of land, their importance cannot be over-emphasized. In the West they ultimately changed the whole pattern of life. Barbed wire (twisted wire with short sharp spikes inserted) came in the late '70s; earlier settlers had used various types of pole fences, including the "Arkansas fence," made of poles stacked in a zigzag pattern.

foreman. Man hired by the owner to manage the operations of his ranch: rounding-up, branding, trail drives, etc.

fork, *v.* To straddle or mount a horse.

Forty-five (pistol). *See* COLT.

Forty-four (pistol). *See* COLT.

free milling rock. Natural rock in which the desired ore is easily separated from the other elements of the rock, i.e., the gangue.

frijoles. Spanish for (dried kidney) *beans,* staple in the diet of Hispanic-Americans of the Southwest.

galoot, *n.* Epithet for a man suggesting age, awkwardness —and a bit of sympathy notwithstanding.

gat. Pistol (from Gatling gun).

Gila monster. *Heloderma suspectum.* This sluggish and retiring creature is the only poisonous lizard in the United States. He stands about five inches high, measures up to twenty inches in overall length, and weighs up to three pounds. Range is the arid portions of the southwestern United States, from southern Utah into Old Mexico. He is nocturnal, prefers rocky areas where his mottled light pink or buff and black body blends with the environment.

ginks. Epithet for nondescript men, idlers, lookers-on.

gopher. *See* PRAIRIE DOG.

gospel sharp, *n.* A preacher; made by analogy to "cardsharp."

grab leather, *v.* When riding a bucking bronc, a cowboy's sense of pride, at least in the presence of his peers, demands that he does not hold onto the saddle with his hands, i.e., that he does not "grab leather." To do so in the bronc riding event at a rodeo disqualifies the rider.

greasers. The Anglo-American's denigrating name for Hispanic-American males of the Southwest.

gringo. Hispanic-Americans' denigrating epithet for Anglo-American men. At least two etymologies have been offered: Spanish *griego,* or Greek, and by extension *gibberish*; and the fusion of the first two words in the refrain of a song widely sung by American soldiers in the Mexican war: "Green grow [hence *gringo*] the lilacs . . ."

grizzly bear. *Ursus horribilis,* a formidable denizen of the Northern Rockies whose range is now restricted to the most remote areas. His almost black fur is silvery and resplendent at the tips. He has a moderate hump over the shoulders, and a slightly swayed back. Specimens weigh up to one thousand pounds. Though basically vegetarian, this formidable and powerful animal is known for horrible deeds of carnage among wild and domestic beasts and, though rarely, among men.

grub pile, *n.* Grub; a synonym for chuck; "Grub pile!" is the camp cook's chuck call.

gunplay, *n.* Applied to the exchange of shots between gunmen, especially the exchange of pistol fire. "To make a play" meant to draw and fire.

hackamore. Spanish *jáquima*, halter. It is usually a halter with reins in lieu of a rope. It was and still is often used instead of a bridle during the early stages of training. It differs from a bridle principally in that, in lieu of bit within the mouth, there is a bosal, i.e., a braided rawhide noose around the horse's muzzle.

hand. *See* COWHAND.

hazers, *n.* Roping, bulldogging, and bronc busting were typically carried out by cowboys working as a team: the hazer's function was to pinch the critter into a position where the roper or dogger could make his play.

heifers. The term "cow" designated cattle of both sexes. A heifer is the female of the species, especially one that has not calved. By extension it meant girls and young women, especially those

participating in a square dance.

high-falutin', *adj.* In this primitivistic reaction to effeminate citified manners, the westerner naturally scorned "high-falutin'" speech and behavior.

hit the rag. Synonym for excessive drinking.

hobbles. Leather cuffs connected with a chain to the forelegs of a horse; the animal, so restrained, can still move enough for a night's grazing. Yet he is sufficiently restricted to be easily located when needed a few hours later.

hog-tie, *v.* Rendering an animal helpless after it is thrown by tying its two hind legs and one front leg together with a short piece of rope. The ties are made with half hitches and the rope used is a small soft one about three feet long. On one end is a loop which the man slips on the foreleg of the downed animal. Standing behind it, with one knee on it to help hold it down, he then sticks his foot under and behind the hocks and boosts the hind legs forward, at the same time drawing the boggin' string under and around both hind feet. This puts the two hind feet on top, pointing forward, and the forefoot below, pointing back. With two or three turns and two half hitches the animal is thoroughly tied. Horses are never hog-tied. (Adams, pp. 77–78.)

hombre. Spanish for *man.* Generally applied by Americans to one of low character, or in conjunction with such adjectives as bad, tough, etc.

horn. On western saddles the pommel is capped by a horn, or a leather-covered protuberance designed to receive a turn or two (i.e., a dally) of the lasso at the instant of its being hurled upon a critter. It has many other practical functions, even including something to hang onto when the going gets tough. But cowboys don't talk about that!

horse. The horse has many names among westerners. In the poems of this collection the following appear:
(1) barb, courser, steed, stallion, nag: these have no peculiar cowboy or western meanings and hence are not defined here.
(2) bronc (bronk, bronco, broncho): from Spanish *bronco,* an adjective meaning rough, coarse, harsh. It is used to designate ungentled or semigentled horses, cowhorses generally, but especially tough, lively, and cantankerous specimens whose behavior matches that of the wild breed of western men. Bronc buster: professional "breaker" of ungentled horses. The art is much more than the mere capacity to stay in the saddle; the bronc buster must also be able to instill some of the discipline and skills that will eventually turn a wild animal into a reliable cowhorse. A bronco steer is a critter so wild that he has antisocial tendencies even among his own kind.
(3) broomtail: shabby range horse, especially a mare.
(4) cayuse: general term for horses, either wild or broken, especially nondescript, unpretentious specimens; said to be derived from the Cayuse Indians of the Northwest.
(5) mustang: in Spanish *mesteño,* derived from *mesta* or a group of horse breeders. It originally referred to the bands of wild horses in the Southwest. Here it means simply a fiery and treacherous cowhorse.
(6) pony, cowpony: general term for a thoroughly gentled but unpretentious horse usable in any job a ranch might demand, even for the use of children or women.

See also OUTLAW, PACKHORSE.

246

hotbox. Railroad cars had metal containers filled with rags saturated in oil at the wheel hubs: when oil was lacking or its flow hampered the hubs heated and emitted a trail of acrid smoke, called a "hotbox."

Injun whiskey. A cheap whiskey used by early Indian traders. Teddy Blue Abbott, who claims it was invented by Missouri River traders, gives the following recipe for it: "Take one barrel of Missouri River water, and two gallons of alcohol. Then you add two ounces of strychnine to make them crazy—because strychnine is the greatest stimulant in the world—and three plugs of tobacco to make them sick —because an Indian wouldn't figure it was whiskey unless it made him sick—five bars of soap to give it a bead, and half-pound of red pepper, and then you put in some sage brush and boil it until its brown. Strain this into a barrel and you've got your Indian whiskey." (Adams, p. 83.)

iron. Horseshoe. *See also* BRAND.

jag, *n.* Drink of whiskey.

jimpson (jumpson) weed. *Datura stramonium,* weed of the tobacco family appreciated by Indians for its narcotic qualities. It has been known to poison cattle, as all parts of the plant contain an atropine alkaloid. It frequently replaces more desirable plants in over-grazed areas. Grows to three feet in height.

J.P. Justice of the Peace.

kinky, *adj.* Whimsical, hence apt to stampede or scatter; said of cattle or women.

lariat. From the Spanish *la reata,* the rope used to tie pack animals in single file. Later extended to mean any rope used in working cattle.

lasso. Portuguese *laco,* noose, *n.* A long rope, usually made of hide, with a running eyelet or *honda* at one end for making a loop. Also used as a verb. Extended at times to mean the wiles women use to subdue a male.

layout. A ranch, or spread; a ranching operation, its components and logistics.

line. *See* RIDE THE LINE.

lion. *See* MOUNTAIN LION.

llanos, *n.* Spanish; Flat, treeless, open prairies.

lobo. Spanish for *wolf.*

loco, n., adj. Spanish, meaning mad, crazy. Species of *astragalus* producing a drug which affects animals, especially horses. Several species are spread widely in the mountain West. The effect is cumulative.

longhorns. A name given to Texas cattle, because of the enormous spread of their horns; also the name for native men of Texas. The saga of the longhorn is interesting, and for a valuable and complete study of this historic bovine, I recommend *The Longhorns,* by an able recorder of the West, J. Frank Dobie (Boston: Little, Brown, 1941). (Adams, p. 93.)

loop. To make a catch with his lasso a roper builds a loop six to eight feet in diameter. This loop is then rotated in a circle above the horse and the roper until the exact moment for the catch comes. Released, the loop extends out and over or under the critter. If it encircles the animal as it should, a dally on the horn and the sudden stopping of the horse cinches the loop up, tightens the rope, and often gives the animal such a wallop that it is thrown off its feet. Rhythm, timing, judgment, and team work of man and mount all

combine to make a spectacle as engaging as the motions of a couple in classical ballet.

macheers. We have not found any other references to this item, which is part of the tack of a saddle horse.

make a play. *See* GUNPLAY.

makin's, n. Cigarette material. The old-time cowboy never smoked any cigarettes other than the ones he rolled himself from his makin's. If he ran out of makin's on the trail, he asked another rider for them and was seldom refused, unless the refusal was an intentional insult. (Adams, p. 96.)

mañana, n. Spanish for *tomorrow*; or *sometime*, perhaps *never.* The word is used freely by Americans along the Mexican border in association with a leisurely postponement. (Adams, p. 96.)

marshal, n. In the United States, an officer of various kinds; specifically: (a) a Federal officer appointed to a judicial district to carry out court orders and perform functions like those of a sheriff; (b) a minor officer of the law; (c) the head of the police or fire department. Here it refers to the local law enforcement officers.

maverick, *n., v.* An unbranded calf of uncertain ownership. As a verb it is the act of placing one's own brand on such an animal. Adams (p. 97) traces it to the name of Samuel E. Maverick, who sold a range herd to a neighbor. Since many of the Maverick cattle were unbranded, the purchaser of the Maverick brand claimed and branded every animal he encountered, including some that did not belong to Maverick: hence *to maverick* came to mean to steal and brand unbranded cattle. By extension rough western young men were also known as *mavericks* and even came to bear the name as a permanent fixture.

mesa. Spanish for *table, tableland,* etc. Usual term applied to the flat-topped mountains or elevated plateaus characteristic of many regions of the Southwest.

mescal. Spanish; liquor made from the *maguey* or century plant (*agave americana*).

mesquite. Spanish *mezquite,* probably of Mexican-Indian origin. A tree or shrub found in the Southwest, especially in the flat country. The wood is exceedingly hard and durable underground. The plant is covered with thorns, and its fruit is a pulpy bean full of grape-sugar which cattle feed on when they can get nothing better. (Adams, p. 99.)

milling. The movement of cattle in a compact circle. This formation is forced upon a herd to stop a stampede. As the cattle mill in a circle, they wind themselves up into a narrowing mass which becomes tighter and tighter until, finally, they can no longer move. When the same action takes place with horses, it is spoken of as *rounding-up,* the term *milling* being reserved strictly for cattle. The milling of cattle on the bedground where they should be lying down was a symptom of restlessness, and forewarning of a stampede.

mogging. Riding slowly along.

monte. A gambling game of Spanish origin, played with a special deck of forty cards, in which the players bet against a banker on the color of cards to be turned up from the deck. It is a nickname often carried by a westerner.

Mormon Bible. In times when the Mormon faith had not achieved respectability "to take a 'davy' on a Mormon Bible" meant to swear an oath on a ludicrous object. It refers specifically to the *Book of Mormon,* of course.

mountain lion. Although there are several species of large cats in cowboy country, the largest and most publicized is *Felis concolor*, which once ranged from Canada to Florida and Old Mexico, even into Central and South America, but is now restricted to very remote areas. Large specimens run up to eight feet in length and weigh up to two hundred pounds. They are tawny colored with tinges of gray, and the long tail ends in a small black tuft. The popular nomenclature is ambivalent and there are regional peculiarities: cougar, puma, panther, painter, or simply lion may serve for this and other members of the western or Mexican cat family.

mustang. *See* HORSE.

nag. *See* HORSE.

nester, *n.* A squatter who settles on state or government land. This term was applied with contempt by the cattlemen of the Southwest to the homesteaders who began tilling the soil in the range country. Viewed from some ridge, the early nester's home looked like a gigantic bird's nest, as he cleared his little patch of brush and stacked it in a circular form to protect his first feed patch from range cattle.

The cowboy, ever quick to catch resemblances, mentioned it to the next man he met, and the name spread and stuck to every man who settled on the plains to till the soil. (Adams, p. 104.)

nigger gin. We have not been able to find any information about this product, However, it was common practice on the frontier to apply the epithet "Indian" or "nigger" to products of inferior quality or dangerous potency.

niggerhead. A black variety of chewing tobacco.

night herd, *n.* On a cattle drive it was necessary to ride circle around the bedded cattle all night long lest they stampede or scatter. Guards spelled each other at two-hour intervals. The night horse was chosen for his keen sight, surefootedness, and unfaltering sense of direction and calm under adverse circumstances. Riding night herd gave a puncher time to speculate about the nature of the cosmos and his personal involvement therein. Night herd songs capture these transcendental experiences in rhythms gauged, like lullabies, to calm the restless cows.

night horse. *See* NIGHT HERD.

noose, *n.* Usually a synonym for loop.

norther, *n.* A driving gale from the north that hurtles over the Southwest, and, coming into collision with preceding warm, moist breezes from the Gulf of Mexico, causes a sudden and extreme drop in temperature. What is called a blizzard in the rest of the West is called a norther in Texas and the Southwest. As one cowhand at Amarillo, Texas, said, "They jes' pour off the North Pole with nothin' to stop 'em but a bob-wire fence and it's full o' knotholes." (Adams, p. 105.)

outfit, *n.* All the hands engaged in a given cattle operation, as a roundup, a trail drive, etc.; the supplies, wagons, gear, equipment, and mounts of such a group; a ranch, together with its herds, buildings, and equipment; wearing apparel.

outlaw. Apart from its usual designation — a westerner who lives by his guns and on theft, plunder, and outright murder — the term is extended to vicious, untamable horses and cows.

owl. Of the many *Bubo* in the West, it is probably the species *virginianus,* or great horned owl, which interested western pioneers the most. He ranges throughout most of North America, has a wingspan up to two feet, and is named for his conspicuous ear tufts. There is also a smaller burrowing owl, *Speotyto cunicularia,* which cohabits with the prairie dogs. It has a wingspread of about nine inches.

pack horse. Punchers, sheepherders, or prospectors going on horseback into remote or relatively inaccessible regions took along, in addition to the "hot roll" tied behind the saddles of their mounts, one or more animals — horse or mule — carrying supplies of all kinds. These pack horses had to be sturdy and tractable, but little else.

pack rat. *See* DESERT RAT.

paint the town red, *v.* A westerner's drunken spree and all that goes with it. *See also* BENDER.

panther. *See* LION.

pard. Cowboys often worked and played in pairs, members of which were known as *pards*, less often *pals*.

pass in his checks (chips), *v.* To die.

picket rope. Used to stake out a horse so that it can graze a bit and still be available for immediate use. On the trail or at a range roundup, special stakes and picket ropes were brought along; the lariat was spared for more essential service.

pick-up, *n.* At a rodeo a buckaroo is usually more than ready to dismount the instant he has stayed on the exact number of seconds required; the *pick-ups* or *pick-up men,* mounted and ready, ride alongside and take him off; they also take the outlaw horse or other critter in hand and get him out of the arena when the ride is over.

pine knots. Outdoorsmen still learn, or should learn, that the resinous knots of various species of evergreens make the best cooking fires because they burn slowly and hot. They are easily gathered in almost any pine forest: they are the last portions of the wood to rot because of their hard resinous makeup.

piñon. One of three open-branched evergreens of the mountain West: *Pinus edulis,* from which pine nuts are harvested; *Pinus monophylla;* and *Pinus cembroides.* The latter is encountered especially in Mexico.

pitching hay. Prior to the advent of farm and ranch mechanization, pitching hay was one of the most dreary muscle jobs on a ranch. Hay that had been mowed, dried, and raked into piles was bunched, i.e., thrown into rows of small piles with a hand fork, then pitched on flat-bedded wagons known as hay racks. Hauled to the stacker or barn, it then was lifted by derrick and "Jackson fork" upon the stack where it was dropped and stacked (again by a man with a pitchfork) so as to shed water and thus be available for winter feeding. Winter feeding more or less reversed the process, with an equal amount of pitching.

pizen (poison). Slang for whiskey.

placer gold. Gold eroded from its original bedrock location and dropped in water or glacial deposits of sand, gravel, or silt. As the baser materials were washed away in pan or sluice, the flakes of gold sparkled "like Val Berry's yaller hair," if we may reverse the image of one of the ballads of this collection.

plug tobacco. Chunks of tobacco, pressed into bars and sold for chewing, were known as *plugs.* Other tobacco lacking, a puncher might shred his plug tobacco and smoke it.

poison, *n.* See the less elegant but more authentic PIZEN.

poke, *n.* Purse.

poker, *n.* For a learned and literate description of the westerner's favorite card game we urge you to read the poem under that title, Number 97 of this collection.

pony, cowpony. *See* HORSE.

posse. Band of riders assembled by an officer of the law to track down and apprehend an outlaw.

pound leather, *v.* To ride, usually at a fast clip.

prairie dog (gopher). Several burrowing rodents of the genus *Cynomys* which are confined to areas of moderate rain. They breed in colonies, building mounds that are dangerous to running cattle and cowponies, for if the hoof should penetrate down into the burrow a fall and almost inevitable injury are in store for both mount and rider.

prickly pear. General term applied to cacti of the genus *opuntia,* characterized by flattened stems: widely spread from Montana south.

prod, on the. A steer, "full of piss and vinegar," and hence ready either to do battle with his kin or take off across lots to hell was said to be "on the prod."

punch, *v.* To punch cows is a general term covering all of a puncher's direct work with cattle—driving, roping, branding, cutting, ear-marking, etc. By extension and a bit derisively punching dough (i.e., kneading dough) covered the camp cook's work with food.

puncher. Usual name for a man who worked with cattle. It is said to derive from the necessity of prodding cattle which lie down in a railroad car: they must be kept on their feet to avoid being trampled by the other cattle.

quaking aspen (asp). *Populus tremuloides,* a beautiful white-barked poplar with leaves that tremble in the slightest breeze. It grows in the West in compact groves called clones. The bark is frequently subjected to carving of names, initials, brands, and various other figures: each clone, hence, carries a record of its own human history.

quirt. In Spanish, *cuerda,* cord; becomes Mexican *cuarta,* meaning whip. It consists of

253

a wooden or leaded stock braided over with rawhide tapered into three or four loose rawhide thongs. The stock may be used as a blackjack, or to pacify horses that tend to rear. A loop in the butt of the stock serves to anchor it on the rider's wrist or the saddle.

ranch. From the Spanish *rancho*. A farm, especially one devoted to the breeding and raising of livestock. Note also: rancher, ranchman, ranch hand, etc. The "home ranch in the skies" appears as an image of life after death.

range. Unfenced country where cattle graze. In U.S. public surveying, one of the north-south rows of townships lying between two consecutive meridian lines, six miles apart, and numbered east and west from the principal meridian of each survey. It is in this latter sense that the word is used in the famous "Home on the Range" song. The term is extended to mean death (i.e., to change ranges), or the hereafter.

ranger. One of a body of mounted troops for patrolling a region. *See* TEXAS RANGERS.

rat. *See* DESERT RAT.

rattlesnake (rattler). Several species of poisonous reptiles of the *Crotalidae* family are widely distributed in the United States. Most typical in cowboy country was *Crotalus viridis,* or the prairie rattler, of which there are several subspecies. They grow to three feet in length; their range extends from Alberta into Old Mexico, and from the western plains states to the Pacific Coast. The diamond back, *Crotalus astrox*, has a more southern range (from Arkansas south and west to Old Mexico). It is much larger, up to eight feet in length, and more deadly: the name is derived from a distinctive patterning along its back.

raven. *Corvus corax* is a large black scavenger which ranges widely across the United States and Canada. He is also known to prey on the eggs and young of less powerful species.

rawhide. Many frontier crafts depended upon use of the tanned hides of cattle: ropes, chaps, saddles, horsegear, chair seats, clothing, and other items were contrived by the use of rawhide. Appears also as a place name.

reata, *n.* Spanish. *See* LARIAT.

254

rebosa, also *rebozo.* Spanish; scarf or long shawl worn over the head and shoulders of Mexican women.

red-eye. Slang for whiskey.

rein chains. Hispanic-American horsemen often used bridle reins which were attached to the bit by a silver or gold chain about one foot long. It may have been practical, in that the leather of reins near the mouth deteriorated rapidly because of prolonged exposure to saliva.

rep, *n.* A man who represents his brand at outside ranches during a general roundup. He is usually at the top of the cowboy profession and is a riding encyclopedia on brands and earmarks. His work is done in following the round-ups on other ranges and turning back strays of his brand. His eye is so well trained that he can discover cattle belonging to his outfit in a vast, milling herd through a dust fog. Also, "to build a rep," i.e., to perform in a manner to induce admiration and respect.

ride the line, *v.* When ranges were unfenced cattle could wander miles, defying the common law that circumscribed the range for each brand. The line rider's job was to patrol these unfenced boundaries, to push strays off his own boss's terrain, and to return his own brand to its proper grazing area. He rode alone and often didn't make it back to his guitar and bunkhouse at night.

rimming, *v.* To ride circle on a herd so that their grazing area is restricted within desired limits.

rimrock, *n.* The vertical escarpments of southwestern plateaus, buttes, or mesas are known as the rimrocks; seen from the valley floors, they rise like the architectural remains of a cosmic temple.

roadhouse. Saloon, inn, or tavern in a trail town; also a corral in an out-of-way place used to hold stolen horses or cattle.

rodeo, *n.* From Spanish *rodear*, to surround. In actual ranching operations it was a synonym for roundup, the driving of cattle together for whatever purpose; more recently it is applied to the conventionalized and highly developed "western show" where cowboys compete in riding, roping, and dogging.

roll, *n.* Cowhands on trail herd were typically paid in cash. The greenbacks were rolled up and carried in the hip

255

pocket. The demonstrative way in which the puncher drew out his roll and peeled off his cash was no doubt a temptation for cardsharps and prostitutes in the trail head towns.

rope, *n., v.* The cowhand's rope was the very sustenance of life itself—weapon and slave. With it he captured animals, both domestic and wild; he dragged firewood to camp, staked his horses, dueled, tied his packs. As a verb it meant to do almost anything you could with a rope, especially to rope cattle. Syn. *lasso.* In a square dance it meant to join hands for a new figure.

roper, *n.* Term applied generally to punchers who did the roping at a roundup. At a modern rodeo, roping and dogging are frequently done in teams: when the critter leaves the chute, roper or dogger and hazer ride out on either side, pinching the critter into a position where a proper throw can be made, or where the dogger can descend upon the horns to throw it.

roundup, *n., v.* Probably derived by translation from the Spanish *rodeo*, action of surrounding. This represented the cattleman's annual harvest; the image of a gathering of folks for a cowboy dance;

and was also used transcendentally as a symbol of death.

rowel. "Business end" of a spur consisting of a dentated rotating wheel; rowel-less spurs had a rigid prong in lieu of a wheel.

rustle, *v.* To herd the *remuda;* to steal cattle; and by extension, to choose partners at a dance. Rustler is one who steals cattle, and is extended to mean sinner.

saddle, full-stamped. A saddle covered with fancy stamped designs. These hand-tooled saddles are not merely to satisfy a rider's ego. The rough indentations cause a friction between the leather and the rider's smooth trouser legs, allowing him to sit tight in the saddle without the tiresome cramping of his legs that result from riding a fractious horse with a smooth saddle. (Adams, p. 63.) By contrast, a "slick" saddle has no stamped surfaces; it may also designate a saddle which has no roll, i.e., no blanket tied behind the fork to help wedge the buckaroo in place.

sagebrush. *Artemisia tridentata.* Typical vegetation of the arid and semiarid West. It adapts to many climatic conditions and serves as food for the larger mammals, especially sheep.

sage hen. *Centrocirius urophasianus.* Large game birds whose range is tied to the sagebrush on which they feed. They are noted for the use they make of traditional breeding grounds where elaborate ritualistic mating dances are enacted. Used popularly to refer to birds of both sexes.

saloon. The saloon was a western institution wedded to the cowboy myth as bees are to honey. Satisfactions for the cowboys' baser instincts — cards, whiskey, and women — were available. Gunmen met there, quarrelled, and shot it out. News was dispensed and deals made. Almost anything, in fact, that couldn't properly be done in church was apt to transpire in the saloon, and hence it is a fitting locale for the westerner's supreme expression of rugged individualism.

sand burrs. A spreading grass (up to four feet in diameter), *Cenchrus pauciflorus*, which produces a hard pea-sized burr which can be irritating and downright dangerous when, as a practical joke, it is placed under the saddle blanket of an already cantankerous horse!

sego lily. The Utah state flower, *Calochortus nuttallii*, a bulbous member of the lily family which grows in thick beds on semiarid hillsides, especially where overgrazing has killed much of the other vegetation. In the first years of pioneering in the Great Salt Lake Valley the bulb was cooked and eaten. It produces a delicate white blossom with a purple gland on each of its three petals.

señorita. Spanish, a nubile unmarried girl: south-of-the-border beauties who provoked the sentimentality and respect of cowboys, and who abandoned their own hearth and home to run away with lonely Anglo-Americans more often in verse and song than they did in real life.

serape. Spanish *sarape.* A woolen blanket or shawl, often brightly colored, worn as an outer garment in Spanish-American countries.

sheep camp. Range sheep require surveillance twenty-four hours a day. The herder lives in a horse-drawn wagon with a canvas cover. It is equipped with a bed, cook stove, and storage space for food and gear.

sheriff. The principal law enforcement officer in a Western community became an institution and a stereotype. He was a gunman gone legitimate and, though on the side of the law, frequently in song and verse his image is an evil one because he is an adversary to the people's outlaw heroes.

shooting rod (shooting iron), *n.* Slang for gun.

six-gun (six-shooter), *n.* Colloquial name for pistols or revolvers which could be fired six times before reloading. "Six-gun law" reigned in the absence of genuine law and is probably the touchstone to the popularity of the "Western" in all of the popular arts.

slick, *n., adj.* Name for an unbranded animal; also a man who has smooth but dishonest ways, especially an outsider. *Slicker, n.* A smooth and heartless deceiver of innocent girls. Also, a raincoat resembling an oilskin, used by cowboys; it was carried tied to the cantle drop of the saddle, ready to be worn when needed.

sluice. A sloping trough or flume through which water is run, as in washing gold ore, carrying logs, etc.

snuffy, *adj.* Of cattle, especially calves, that are wild and spirited; the ones most apt to incite a stampede.

sombrero. The Spanish *sombra* (shade) gave rise to *sombrero,* a hat, especially one that casts plenty of shade. Such hats became a "tag" of the cowboy's gear. Though movie and TV specimens exaggerate both crown and brim, a cowhand found a good hat extremely useful: as a barrier to sun and rain, as protection against twigs and leaves, even as a temporary basin for water. Like his boots and Levi's, it is one of the tags of the cowboy's mythical identity.

Spanish dagger. Several species of *Yucca* are popularly identified as Spanish dagger. They flourish in arid regions of the Southwest. These produce a spray of narrow pointed leaves capped with a sharp spine and a blossom which cattle find edible; grows up to five feet in height.

Spanish moss. An epyphite, *Tyllandsia usneoides,* which roots itself in the branches of evergreen or deciduous trees, especially in east Texas. It produces a stalk with a burst of leaves at the top.

spurs. Metal instruments worn on cowboys' boots to assist in controlling the mount. They became an essential piece of cowboy equipment seldom removed from his boots. They may have been more important as a status symbol than for use on the horse. One of the simplest and most commonly used was the "OK" spur. Their silvery shine, ornate designs, and especially the jingle of the rowels as a cowboy walked gave his gait some real *bezazz* and caused the hearts of impressionable maidens to flip-flop.

squaw man, *n.* Frontiersmen who married squaws, or otherwise went "native," were not highly esteemed in Anglo-American communities.

stage. The horse-drawn stages of the West are one of its favorite stereotyped images. The driver or skinner urges the four-horse team on at a dead run with a flood of vile oaths; the guard beside him, Winchester in hand, scans the countryside for badmen. Among the paying passengers must be found a noble youth, a provocative female, a leering no-good, and a gospel sharp. Before the ride is over there must be an encounter with Indians, or a robbery by Black Bart or some other colorful outlaw.

stampede. From the Spanish *estampida,* the running of cattle. Cattle raised on the open ranges were wild animals. Any sudden noise or other unusual occurrence might set them in a mad run, dangerous to man and beast. Many western songs and stories tell of the drama, excitement, and tragedy of cattle (or buffalo) stampedes. The meaning of the term is extended to include the rush of men to mining strikes.

Stetson, *n.* Name given by Westerners to the big hat that is an earmark of the cattle country, whether made by Stetson or not. Adams (pp. 155–56) gives two full columns to its composition, ornamentation, tilt, practical uses, and symbolic meanings.

stray, *n.* Used to designate cattle grazing on a range where they don't belong. Ethics called for their being headed back toward their own grazing area. If, however, a range crew just happened to be fresh out of meat, and if a stray just happened to be handy, its life was not nearly as secure as was that of a cow bearing the home brand.

strike, *n.* Mining term used to designate the discovery of a rich new source of ore.

stud, *n.* Variety of poker in which each player is dealt five cards, the first face down and the others face up, the betting proceeding as each open card is dealt.

suggans. Blankets for bedding; heavy comforters often made from patches of pants, coats, or overcoats. A suggan usually weighs about four pounds, as the cowboy says, "a pound for each corner." Also called *soogans* or *soogins,* camp quilts, boys' room quilts.

sull, *v.* Cowmen use this word to describe the action of a cow which, in a state of shock or exhaustion, goes down on its front knees and refuses to move.

sunfishing, *v.* A bucking term used in describing the movements of a horse when he twists his body into a crescent, alternately to the right and to the left; or, in other words, when he seems to try to touch the ground with first one shoulder and then the other, letting the sunlight hit his belly.

tapaderos. Spanish; Hispanic-American horsemen attached leather guards known as *tapaderos* in front of the stirrups to prevent the feet from penetrating too far. They also protected the feet against brush and prevented the dreaded tragedy of being dragged to death when, on being thrown, one's foot slip-

ped all the way through the stirrup. Anglo-Americans shortened the term to "taps."

tarp. Canvas in which a puncher rolled bedding and the few personal effects which he carried, tied behind his saddle whenever away from the home ranch. It also served as a waterproof cover on his bed.

tenderfoot, *n.* According to Adams (p. 164), it was first applied to cattle imported to the Southwest, later to men new to the region. *Syn. greenhorn, greener, dude.*

tequila. Spanish. Alcoholic beverage distilled from the juice of the century plant.

Texas Rangers. By 1826 Texas colonists had from twenty to thirty "rangers" in service against Indians. By 1840 an organized corps had come into being: it achieved fame in the war with Mexico. By 1870 it had reached its zenith, imposing order on the Rio Grande in operations against Indians, horse thieves, outlaws, and disorders of the Reconstruction years. They carried six-shooters and saddle guns but were otherwise un-uniformed. They did not drill, their guns were never notched, there was no saluting of officers. —J. Frank Dobie in the *Dictionary of American History,* 2nd ed., Vol. V, pp. 256–57.

tlaco. Spanish. Coin, one-eighth of a Spanish *real;* obsolete.

top hand (man, rider, roper, cutter, screw, shot, etc.), *n.* The best; the man who excels in and is, hence, in charge of a particular punching activity.

tortilla. Spanish. "A large, round, thin, unleavened cake prepared from a paste made of corn, baked on a heated iron plate or stone slab; used in lieu of bread in Mexico."— Webster.

trading post. From the founding of Jamestown (1607), furs were exchanged for guns, ammunition, hatchets, knives, blankets, etc. In 1796 the U.S. government established trading posts, and frontier military outposts became centers of trade between the Indians and the Anglo-American colonists. After the Louisiana Purchase (1803), they were established over a wide expanse of the area west of the Mississippi. They persist today on the Indian reservations, where the Indians procure a wide variety of manufactures, and where tourists buy the products of Indian craftsmanship. —*Dictionary of American History,* 2nd ed., Vol. V, p. 302.

trail drive, *n.* Perhaps the most dramatic of all cowboy activities. Drives over great distances began in the 1830s and continued into the 1880s. Driven hard during the first day or so in order to get them off the home range, the cattle were subsequently trailed easily along so that they could graze and put on fat en route. The work of trail driving was highly organized, with riders cooperating as skillfully as the members of a professional athletic team. The cattle were known as the trail herd.

tumble weed. *Amaranthus graecizans* or *Salsola kali* (Russian thistle). Annual weeds which break off at the root at the end of the growing season and which, because of spheroid shape, blow across the country, scattering their seeds and piling up on every fence line. They came into the West from Eurasia, where they were eaten as greens and their seeds ground for flour. Some reach a diameter of six feet.

"Turn out there!" One of the camp cook's duties, on trail drive or roundup, was to get the hands up, fed, and mounted. Each had his favorite "gettin' up holler" or chuck call, some of which can be repeated in print.

vaquero. Spanish for *cowboy.* The term gives rise in cowboy lingo to buckaroo, admitting contamination from the verb *buck.* (Recall that an initial *v* in Spanish is pronounced like a *b.*) In all probability, it served to fix the term *cowboy,* which is a faithful translation of *vaca* (cow), and *ero,* a suffix meaning a person who deals with something.

waddies. Name for ordinary cowboys, usually those who floated from ranch to ranch, who were engaged for seasonal work only. Adams (p. 173) thinks it may be derived from *wad,* i.e., something you use to temporarily stop a leak until you can do the job up good and proper.

wagon boss. Man in charge of a roundup or trail drive; undisputed leader of an operating outfit. The movies have glorified the wagon bosses who piloted groups of pioneers in wagon trains.

wire grass. *Junicus balticus,* a worthless blue-green grass which produces coarse stalks up to eighteen inches high, appearing typically in wet meadows.

wolf. *Canis lupus* once ranged widely in North America, though he is now restricted to the most remote areas. He is about the size of an Alaskan husky dog, weighing up to one hundred twenty pounds. Pioneers were fearful of them, especially because they roved in packs and preyed alike upon domestic or wild animals, even the most hardy ones. Two other species, *Canis occidentales,* or the timber wolf, and *Canis ladrans,* the prairie wolf or coyote, were probably not always differentiated by the folk who used the term *wolf* for largest specimens and *coyote* for the smaller ones.

wrangler, wrangle. From the Mexican *caverango,* or hostler. Man on roundup or trail drive who took care of the *remuda,* typically the least experienced hand in the outfit. It is extended to mean the performance of the duties of camp cook, and to the restless milling of cattle.

"yip!" (with variations). Cries and shouts used by punchers to get the cattle moving in a desired direction; prettied-up and stereotyped, they serve well in the refrains of western songs and verse.

———————

Indices

Titles and First Lines

[First lines are set in italics; titles are set in roman type]

General Index

The body text for *Ballads of the Great West* is Times Roman, and the chapter heads are Trump Medieval Bold, both set in Linofilm by Applied Typographic Systems, Palo Alto, California. The book was printed by Peninsula Lithograph Company, Menlo Park, California and bound by The Cardoza Bookbinding Company, San Francisco, California. The paper is Capstan Vellum, cream white, and the cloth is Holliston Roxite, linen finish.

Illustrations by Glen Rounds.

Design by John Beyer.